Intermediate Infor[illegible] Technology

CW01643143

This book is
the la

STOKE ON TRENT COLLEGE
A048380
FC

PROPERTY OF
STOKE-ON-TRENT
COLLEGE

Intermediate Information Technology

Joyce Mount

Lecturer in Office Technology
South Cheshire College

Stoke-on-Trent College
LIBRARY
WITHDRAWN
15 FEB 1996
004.6
MOU
Burslem Campus

McGRAW-HILL BOOK COMPANY

London · New York · St Louis · San Francisco · Auckland
Bogotá · Caracas · Hamburg · Lisbon · Madrid · Mexico · Milan
Montreal · New Delhi · Panama · Paris · San Juan · São Paulo
Singapore · Sydney · Tokyo · Toronto

A048380

Published by
McGRAW-HILL Book Company Europe
Shoppenhangers Road, Maidenhead, Berkshire, SL6 2QL, England
Telephone 0628 23432
Fax 0628 770224

British Library Cataloguing in Publication Data
Mount, Joyce
Intermediate Information Technology
I. Title
004

ISBN 0–07–707604–4

Copyright © 1992 McGraw-Hill International.
All rights reserved. No part of this publication may be reproduced, stored in a retrieval system, or transmitted, in any form or by any means, electronic, mechanical, photocopying, recording, or otherwise, without the prior permission of McGraw-Hill International.
12345 95432
Printed and bound in Great Britain

To Phil

CONTENTS

NOTE TO TUTORS AND STUDENTS

The following are required as extracts for the unit on the collating of information. It is therefore necessary to either keep an additional copy of the printout or to save the extract/graph on disk depending upon the method of collation used.

PAGE NO	TASK NO
6	9
10	8
13	6
13	7
14	10
19	2
20	6
30	17
79	4
80	6
82	4
84	5

UNIT 1

DATABASES

For this unit you will need to know how to set up and manipulate a database.

DO YOU KNOW ?

How to set up a database?

The different types of fields?

How to determine the field description?

How to enter the record structure?

How to select the relevant data?

How to enter the data?

The most logical way of entering the data?

How to sort the records into alphabetical/numerical order?

How to search on three criteria to select a subset?

How to print an entire database?

How to print selected fields in a subset?

How to save the data?

As each of these points are needed, you will be told at the beginning of the section, so that you can either learn how to carry out the function or refresh your memory.

HINTS AND TIPS

1 Read the instructions carefully about the data to be included. To include too much or too little will result in a penalty for selecting the relevant data, objective 1.1.

2 Make sure that the field is wide enough to enter all the data, without abbreviations (unless these are required).

3 Make sure that all data entry errors are corrected *before* printing.

4 The data must be entered in a consistent manner, eg if the name is to be entered SURNAME (in capitals), FIRST NAME (in full), eg SMITH John Graham - all names must be entered in the same way. If data is not entered consistently the sort facility may not produce the correct sequence.

5 A search on three criteria is always required, make sure that after making the search, the correct fields are printed. A selection of fields, or all fields may be required - check the instructions carefully.

6 Always key in field data in the same way, ie all capitals or initial capital and lower case letters. A mixture may influence the sorting/searching facilities.

7 When printing the file, choose the type size which will fit the document onto one page, ie choose condensed print if possible for a wide file.

ASSIGNMENT 1

For this set of tasks you will need Source Documents A for Sierra Car Hire (pages 98 - 102).

DO YOU KNOW? **How to set up a database?**
How to determine the type of field?
How to enter the record structure?

Task 1

Set up a database for a car hire firm using the following fields:

SURNAME
GROUP OF CAR
MODEL OF CAR
NO OF DAYS
DEPOSIT
BALANCE DUE
PREMIUM
PICK UP
DROP OFF

DO YOU KNOW? How to extract the relevant data?
How to enter the data?

Task 2

Enter the data into the database, extracting the relevant information from the Source Documents. Save the file.

DO YOU KNOW? How to print the whole file?
How to print a file in condensed script?

Task 3

Print one copy of the database, showing all fields.

DO YOU KNOW? How to sort a file?

Task 4

Sort the database into alphabetical order of surname and print a copy showing all fields.

DO YOU KNOW? **How to search on one criterion?**

How to print selected fields?

Task 5

Extract the records for those hirers who have paid the insurance premium. Print surname, group of car and number of days hired.

DO YOU KNOW? **How to search on two criteria?**

Task 6

Extract the records for those hirers who have hired a Group C car for more than 10 days. Print surname, deposit, balance due and whether or not the insurance premium was paid.

DO YOU KNOW? **How to search on three criteria?**

Task 7

Extract the records for those hirers who have hired an Excelsior car, who have not paid the insurance premium and who wish to pick up the car at the airport. Print surname, number of days and deposit paid.

Task 8

Sort the file into ascending order of number of days. Print surname, group of car, pick up and drop off points.

Task 9

Extract the records for those hirers who have hired a Pyramid car and who wish to pick up their cars at the airport and drop them off at the hotel. Print all fields.

DO YOU KNOW? How to make amendments to an existing database?

Task 10

Make the following amendments to the data already keyed in:

Margaret Channon's name should be Marguerita.

Barbara Culhane has decided to pick up her car at the airport and drop it off at the hotel.

Moubarak Massin has decided to change to a Pyramid 2.0, Group C car. Find out from the other records what the costs are, and make the necessary amendments.

Task 11

Print the revised database showing all fields.

DO YOU KNOW? How to delete records?

Task 12

Pamela Elsworth and Roger Hannon have decided not to hire the car and have had their deposits refunded. Delete the records.

Task 13

Sort the revised database into alphabetical order of surname. Print one copy showing all fields.

DO YOU KNOW? How to save your original database file?
How to delete any subfiles you have created?
How to make back-up copies of your database file?
How to format a disk?

Task 14

Save the original database file. Delete all subfiles which you may have created. Make a back-up copy of the original database file on to a newly formatted disk or on to a different user area.

The printouts for the tasks marked with an asterisk are needed for use in the later collated documents. Retain these printouts for future use.

ASSIGNMENT 2

For this set of tasks you will need Source Documents B for Sierra Theatre Bookings (pages 103 - 7).

Task 1

Set up a database for a theatre bookings agency using the following fields:

NAME
TOWN
SHOW
DATE
TYPE OF SEATS
ADULTS
CHILDREN
PAYMENT BY
AMOUNT
CREDIT CARD NO
EXPIRY DATE

NOTES:

(1) The expiry date on a credit card is normally shown as month/year, eg 06/93. For this database, enter the month as given followed by next year, eg in 1992 enter 06/93.

(2) Enter the name as shown on the data sheet, ie surname followed by first name.

Task 2

Enter the data into the database extracting the relevant data from Source Documents B - Sierra Theatre Bookings.

Task 3

Print one copy of the file showing all fields.

Task 4

Sort the file into alphabetical order of surname. Print one copy showing all fields.

Task 5

Sort the file into descending order of expiry date of credit card. Print one copy showing all fields.

Task 6

Extract the records for those people who have booked seats in the stalls. Print one copy showing the name of the person booking the tickets, and the name of the show they have booked for.

Task 7

Extract the records for those people who have booked tickets for Liverpool plays. Print one copy showing the following fields: show, type of seats, number of adults, number of children.

Task 8

Extract the records for those people who have paid for their bookings by credit card. Print one copy showing the following fields: name, amount, credit card number, expiry date.

Task 9

Extract the records for those people who have booked for *The Tempest*, and print one copy showing the following fields: name, date, type of seats.

Task 10

Extract the records for those people who have booked stall seats for *Julius Caesar* and who have booked for less than five children. Print one copy showing the following fields: name, payment, number of adults.

Task 11

Extract the records for those people who have booked circle seats for shows in Liverpool for adults only. Print one copy showing the following fields: name, name of show, date of show.

Task 12

Extract the records for those people who have booked balcony seats for Manchester shows and have paid by credit card. Print one copy showing the following fields: name, amount, credit card number, expiry date.

Task 13

Make the following amendments to the data already keyed in:

Abdul Shawani has changed his mind and would like to have balcony seats. The amount to be charged to his credit card is £44.

Angus Doyle wants the same tickets, but for one week later, ie 30/1.

Arthur Lee has changed his mind, and wishes to pay by credit card. His card number is 727 513 861 231. Expiry date 11/.

The performances for Ellesmere Port have been relocated to Birkenhead following a fire at the theatre. Find all records and make the necessary changes.

Edward Bradbourne states that his surname has been spelt incorrectly.

Ian Cropper paid by credit card, but gave an incorrect expiry date - it should be 8/.

W M Ellison rang to inform us that his tickets had been sent to the incorrect address. His address should read 164 Teveret Close.

Task 14

Print one copy of the revised file showing all fields. Mark with a pencil the corrections you have made.

Task 15

Extract all records for those people who have booked seats for the Ellesmere Port shows which have been relocated to Birkenhead. Print the names and addresses so that they can be informed of the change and asked if they wish to have a refund on their tickets.

ASSIGNMENT 3

For this set of tasks you will need Source Documents C for Sierra Property Company (pages 108 - 17).

Task 1

Set up a database for an estate agent, giving details of purchasers looking for specific properties. Use the fields indicated, and abbreviate *sensibly* if necessary.

NAME
POSTCODE
TEL NO
TOWN
MINIMUM PRICE
MAXIMUM PRICE
TYPE OF PROPERTY
BEDROOMS
RECEPTION ROOMS
GARDEN

Use the following abbreviations for the type of property:

SDH = Semi-detached house
DH = Detached house
TH = Terraced house
F = Flat
SDB = Semi-detached bungalow
DEB = Detached bungalow
DOB = Dormer bungalow

Use the following abbreviations for the type of garden:

L = Large
S = Small
N = None

Task 2

Enter the data into the database, extracting the relevant information from the source documents. When entering the name, enter SURNAME first in capitals followed by other names as given in source documents with initial capital only, eg CANNELL Terence.

Task 3

Print one copy of the file showing all fields. Use condensed print if necessary.

Task 4

Sort the file into alphabetical order of surname and print one copy of all fields.

Task 5

Sort the file into descending order of maximum price and print one copy of all fields.

Task 6

Extract the records of those people who are looking for flats and print one copy of all fields.

Task 7

Extract the records of those people who are looking for properties with large gardens and print one copy of all fields.

Task 8

Extract the records of those people who are looking for properties with a maximum price of £65,000. Print name, telephone number and type of property.

Task 9

Extract the records of those people who are looking for three-bedroomed detached houses. Print name, town, minimum and maximum price.

Task 10

Extract the records of those people who are looking for two-bedroomed semi-detached houses with small gardens and with a minimum price of less than £35,000. Print name, telephone number and town.

Task 11

Sort the file into ascending order of minimum price. Print name, telephone number and minimum price.

Task 12

Extract the records of those people who wish to purchase a property of £65,000 and over. Print all fields.

Task 13

Since entering the initial data, a number of corrections need to be made because purchasers have changed their requirements. Make the following changes:

Karen Jukes no longer requires mortgage facilities.

John Holycroft has raised his maximum price by £10,000.

James Harrison has decided he would like a large garden, and has therefore raised his maximum price by £5,000.

Terence Cannell would now like two reception rooms.

Anne-Marie Glennard would like to change the town to Princeton.

Christine Haggett's surname should be Haget.

Henry Ingersen has raised the minimum price by £10,000 and the maximum price by £7,500.

Stanley Kavanagh lives in Bogner Close not Bognor Close.

Gwynneth Llewellyn would like two reception rooms.

Simon Owen lives in Brander Road not Braddon Road.

Task 14

Print one copy of the revised file showing all fields. Use condensed print if necessary. Mark the corrected fields on the printout with a ruled line.

Task 15

Sort the revised database into alphabetical order of surname. Print one copy showing all fields.

Task 16

Save both the database files. Delete any subfiles you may have created. Keep the copies of the printouts for the tasks required for use with the collated documents. (See the list in the Note to tutors and students.)

UNIT 2

SPREADSHEETS

For this unit you will need to know how to set up and manipulate a spreadsheet.

DO YOU KNOW ?

How to analyse given information into individual categories?

How to enter a spreadsheet layout?

How to change the format of cells from integer to 1, 2 or 3 decimal places?

How to right justify figures?

How to present dates?

How to present monetary items?

How to enter the data?

What a formula is?

How to generate and apply formulae?

How to print the formulae?

How to print the whole spreadsheet or selected cells?

How to display a spreadsheet to the best advantage - showing all figures clearly and consistently?

How to insert rows and columns?

How to generate What If? projections?

How to save the spreadsheet for future use?

As each of these points are needed, you will be told at the beginning of the section, so that you can either learn how to carry out the function or refresh your memory.

HINTS AND TIPS

1 When requested, make sure that you analyse correctly the information given.

2 Each cell entered should be described in the correct manner, eg numerical or alphabetical, according to the data entered.

3 Use the layout indicated, and where appropriate change the width to accommodate the data. Reasonable abbreviations can be used but it is advisable to change the cell width instead.

4 Numbers need to have the correct decimal places - use the context of the figures to tell you which, eg hours of work should have no decimal places, they should be in integer format.

5 Sums of money should be formatted to two decimal places, unless you are told to put them into integer format.

6 Use the best and smallest formulae to make calculations.

7 Print the formulae requested - this is not necessarily all of them.

8 Print selected cells only - no more and no less than requested. Include headings where they aid understanding.

9 Make sure that if you have used the correct What if? projections.

10 Make sure that you have printed two copies of the spreadsheet extract - one to be used in the collated document.

ASSIGNMENT 1

For this set of tasks you will be introduced to the principles of spreadsheets needed to cope with those included in your final assessment.

The Do You Know sections tell you what you need to know to complete that particular task. If you do not know, refresh your memory.

DO YOU KNOW? **What a column is?**
What a row is?
What a cell is?
How to move about the spreadsheet?
How to move to a specified cell?
What to do if an error is made during keying-in?
How to save a spreadsheet?

Task 1

Key in the spreadsheet exactly as it is shown. Start in Cell A1.

BUDGET				
ITEM	JANUARY	FEBRUARY	MARCH	APRIL
FOOD	30	40	40	40
ELECTRICITY	15	15	15	15
GAS	10	10	10	10
CAR INSURANCE	17	17	17	17
TOTALS				

DO YOU KNOW? **What a formula is?**
The formula for adding cells together?
The formula for subtracting two cells?
The formula for dividing two cells?
The formula for multiplying two cells?
How to replicate a formula?

Task 2

Using the budget spreadsheet created in Task 1, use a formula to find the total for January. Replicate the formula for February, March and April. Print one copy.

DO YOU KNOW? **How to insert new columns?**
How to insert new rows?

Task 3

Using the budget spreadsheet already created, add a new row between Gas and Car Insurance for Telephone. Complete the row by inserting 15 for each of the months.

Insert a new column between MARCH and APRIL using the heading QUARTERLY TOTAL (you may use two lines for this - but if you do remember to insert an additional row for the second line).

In the new column, enter the formula for the total for Food for JANUARY, FEBRUARY and MARCH. Replicate the formula for Electricity, Gas, Telephone and Car Insurance.

Save the spreadsheet. Print one copy.

DO YOU KNOW? How to delete a column?
How to delete a row?

Task 4

Using the budget spreadsheet already created, delete the column headed APRIL and the row entitled Car Insurance. Print one copy.

Task 5

Add a final column headed ANNUAL TOTAL. Use a formula in this column to project the annual total of expenditure - this will be the QUARTERLY TOTAL x 4.

Print one copy.

DO YOU KNOW? How to project new values?

Task 6

You wish to see the effect of a 10 per cent overall increase on your budget. Add a new column between QUARTERLY TOTAL and ANNUAL TOTAL headed INCREASE. Use a formula to project the increase for Food and then replicate the formula for all other rows.

Print one copy.

ASSIGNMENT 2

For this set of tasks you will need the Data Sheet for Sierra Car Hire (page 22).

DO YOU KNOW? **How to extract data from Source Documents?**
How to set out the spreadsheet following the instructions given?
How to print the spreadsheet?

Task 1

1 Prepare a spreadsheet using the following layout:

HEADING: Sierra Car Hire

COLUMN HEADINGS: Name of Car, Group, Day Rate, January Rentals, February Rentals (the word Rentals may be put on a second line).

In the first column under Name of Car, put the following side headings:

Pyramid 1.1
Pyramid 1.6
Pyramid 2.9
Van 100
Van 120
Minibus 7/9 seats
Minibus 11/12 seats
TOTALS

SIERRA CAR HIRE – DATA SHEET

The following data relate to the numbers of cars hired out by Sierra Car Hire over the period January (Column A) and February (Column B).

Name of Car	Group	Day £	A	B	Weekend £	A	B	Week £	A	B
PYRAMID 1.1	A	25	10	12	36	9	9	125	16	12
1.3	A	27	7	9	44	4	7	135	19	16
1.4	B	29	14	12	47	8	6	148	12	10
1.5	B	30	15	11	48	2	5	150	9	14
1.6	B	32	27	21	52	7	6	160	7	11
1.8	C	35	16	12	57	8	10	175	11	16
2.0	C	40	10	8	65	11	7	200	10	8
2.3	C	45	7	7	72	12	12	225	6	12
2.9	D	49	4	6	79	16	3	245	2	5
3.0	E	74	6	2	98	4	2	300	8	5
Vans 100	E	17	19	11	28	6	7	82	4	7
120	E	24	10	16	39	9	3	120	8	10
Minibus 7/9	F	46	9	8	74	3	5	219	6	7
11/12	F	35	13	12	56	4	2	179	4	5

Task 1 (cont)

2 Complete the columns extracting the data from the data sheet included in the assignment.

3 Print a copy of the spreadsheet.

4 Add a new column between January Rentals and February Rentals with a heading January Income.

5 Add a new column after February Rentals with a heading February Income.

6 Find the income for January for the Pyramid 1.1 car by using a formula to multiply the Day Rate and the January Rentals. Put the formula into the January Income column. Replicate the formula for all the other vehicles.

7 Find the income for February for the Pyramind 1.1 car by using a formula as for January above and put the formula into the February Income column. Replicate the formula for all other vehicles.

8 Use a formula to insert the totals for the columns January Rentals, January Income, February Rentals and February Income.

9 Save the spreadsheet.

10 Print one copy.

11 Print one copy of an extract of the spreadsheet showing the Name of the Car and the January and February Income. Make sure that you include the headings as well as the data in your printout.

12 Print a copy of the spreadsheet showing all the formulae.

13 In February, the management considered increasing all prices by 10 per cent. Show the effect on the February income of an increase of 10 per cent. Print an extract showing the Name of the Car and the New Income which would be generated.

14 Save the spreadsheet.

Task 2

1 Prepare a spreadsheet using the following layout:

HEADING: February Rentals

COLUMN HEADINGS:
Name of Car
Day Rate
Number Hired
Weekend Rate
Number Hired
Weekly Rate
Number Hired

In the first column under Name of Car list all vehicles on the data sheet.

Insert a final row heading TOTALS.

2 Complete the columns by extracting the relevant data from the data sheet.

3 Print a copy of the spreadsheet.

4 Three new columns need to be added to show the income from each type of rental. These new columns should be added after each column headed Number Hired and should be headed Daily Income, Weekend Income, Weekly Income.

5 Using a formula, complete these columns working out the Daily Income for the Pyramid 1.1 by multiplying the Day Rate by the Number Hired. Replicate the formula for each of the vehicles hired.

6 Repeat the process for both the Weekend Income and the Weekly Income.

7 Print one copy of the spreadsheet showing the contents.

8 Print one copy of the spreadsheet showing the formulae.

9 Print an extract from the spreadsheet of the Name of Car, Weekly Rate, Number Hired and Weekly Income.

10 Print the formulae only for the above extract.

11 Add a final column to the spreadsheet headed Total Income.

12 Use a formula to find the Total Income for all types of hiring - add the Daily, Weekend and Weekly Income for the Pyramid 1.1 car and replicate the formula for the remainder of the vehicles.

13 Print an extract of the Name of Car and Total Income for all vehicles.

14 The management would like to see the result of an increase in price for all hirings of 15 per cent. Add a final column headed Revised Income and use a formula to find the New Income for the Pyramid 1.1 car - replicate the formula for the remainder of the vehicles.

15 Print an extract of the Name of Car, Total Income and Revised Income for all vehicles. Include the headings.

16 Print an extract of the Name of Car, Total Income and Revised Income for the Minibuses only. Include the headings.

17 Print an extract of the Name of Car, Total Income and Revised Income for the Minibuses only, showing only the formulae. Include the headings.

18 The management have asked you to produce the figures for the number of vehicles hired. Print an extract of the data showing the Name of the Car and the Number Hired.

19 In a new section of the spreadsheet, produce a separate spreadsheet by copying the following columns and renaming the column headings:

Name of Car, Number Hired Daily, Number Hired Weekend, Number Hired Weekly - you may put the column headings on more than one line if you wish. Print a copy of that section of the spreadsheet.

20 Add a further column to this section of the spreadsheet to find the average number of vehicles hired. Use the heading Average Hirings. Use a formula to add the three columns together and divide by 3. Print a copy of this section of the spreadsheet.

ASSIGNMENT 3

For this set of tasks you will need the Data Sheet for Sierra Theatre Bookings.

Task 1

1 Prepare a spreadsheet using the following layout:

HEADING: Sierra Theatre Bookings

COLUMN HEADINGS:
Stalls
Tempest
Macbeth
Othello
Julius Caesar
TOTALS

In the column headed Stalls, enter the following row headings:
Price for Adults
No Sold January
No Sold February
Price for Children
No Sold January
No Sold February

2 Complete the columns by extracting the relevant data from the Data Sheet opposite.

3 Print one copy of the spreadsheet.

SIERRA THEATRE BOOKINGS

The following data relates to the numbers of tickets sold by Sierra Theatre Bookings for the four productions in the North West during January and February. The data is divided into types of seats, and the tickets sold for adults and children.

Seats	The Tempest	Macbeth	Othello	Julius Caesar
STALLS				
COST – Adults £	15	20	17	20
SOLD – January	100	123	87	96
SOLD – February	90	100	92	110
COST – Children £	8	12	10	12
SOLD – January	250	247	102	118
SOLD – February	160	171	165	256
CIRCLE				
COST – Adults £	12	15	13	15
SOLD – January	95	146	95	72
SOLD – February	170	212	101	149
COST – Children £	7	9	8	9
SOLD – January	182	132	72	84
SOLD – February	300	196	178	212
BALCONY				
COST – Adults £	10	12	10	12
SOLD – January	150	84	60	163
SOLD – February	142	102	71	111
COST – Children £	6	7	6	7
SOLD – January	201	161	92	212
SOLD – February	276	175	85	178

Task 1 (cont)

4 Insert a row between No Sold January and No Sold February for Adults with the heading Total Income.

5 Use a formula to calculate the income received from *The Tempest* - multiply the price by the number sold. Replicate the formula for *Macbeth, Othello* and *Julius Caesar.*

6 Insert a row between No Sold February and Price for Children with the heading Total Income.

7 Repeat the procedure given in Step 5.

8 Repeat the above procedures for calculating Total Income from adults' seats to produce the income from children's seats.

9 Save the spreadsheet and print one copy.

10 Print a copy showing the formulae used.

11 In the final column headed TOTALS, use a formula to add all rows headed No Sold and Total Income.

12 Add a final row headed TOTALS, and use a formula to give the income for all plays by adding the figures from the cells under each play headed Total Income.

13 Save the spreadsheet.

14 Print two copies of the spreadsheet, one showing the contents of the cell and one showing the formulae.

15 The management wish to know what effect a price increase of 10 per cent will have on the income for the plays. Add a final column headed PLUS 10 per cent and use a formula to calculate the new income.

16 Print a copy of the spreadsheet which shows the following columns: Stalls, Total Income and PLUS 10 per cent.

17 Print a second copy of the extract for step 16 showing the formulae only.

Task 2

1 Prepare a spreadsheet using the following layout:
HEADING: January Sales for Adults
COLUMN HEADINGS: Play, Stalls, Circle, Balcony
ROW HEADINGS under Play: The Tempest, Macbeth, Othello, Julius Caesar, Totals

2 Extract the data from the data sheet and complete the columns and rows.

3 Save the spreadsheet. Print one copy of the spreadsheet.

4 Insert three new columns - one between each column each with the column heading Cost.

5 Extract the data from the data sheet and complete the columns.

6 Save the spreadsheet and print one copy.

7 Add three more columns between Stalls and Cost, Circle and Cost and after Balcony headed Income Stalls, Income Circle, Income Balcony.

8 Use a formula to generate the Stalls Income for *The Tempest* and replicate the formula for the remainder of the plays. Repeat the procedure for the Circle Income and for the Balcony Income.

9 Add a final column headed Overall Totals.

10 Use a formula to generate the Overall Total Income of Stalls, Circle and Balcony for *The Tempest*. Replicate the formula for the remainder of the plays.

11 Print two copies of the spreadsheet, one showing the formulae and one showing the contents.

12 Use a formula to generate the Totals of the number of seats sold for the Stalls, Circle and Balcony, together with the Overall Totals.

13 Print two copies of the spreadsheet, one showing the formulae and one showing the contents.

14 Print an extract from the spreadsheet showing the columns headed Play, Cost, Balcony and Income Balcony.

15 Using a different part of the spreadsheet, copy the columns headed Play, Cost, Balcony and Income Balcony.

16 The management would like to know what effect a price decrease of 15 per cent for the balcony seats would have on the income. Add a final column headed 15 per cent Decrease and use a formula to generate the new income for *The Tempest*. Replicate the formula for the other plays.

17 Print two copies of the spreadsheet extract, one showing the formulae and the other the contents of the cells.

18 Using a different part of the spreadsheet, copy the columns headed Play, Income Stalls, Income Circle, Income Balcony and Overall Totals.

19 Add a final column headed 10 per cent Increase. Use a formula to show the effect of a 10 per cent increase on the overall totals for *The Tempest* and put the result in the new column. Replicate the formula for all other plays.

20 Add a final row to this extract headed Totals. Use a formula to generate the income from stalls. Replicate the formula for the other columns.

21 Save the spreadsheet. Print two copies, one showing the formulae and the other showing the contents.

UNIT 3

WORD PROCESSING

For this unit, you will need to know a number of word processing functions.

DO YOU KNOW ?

How to create a document?

How to save a document?

How to print a multi-page document?

How to set a specified line length?

How to justify the right margin?

How to edit the text as you key-in?

How to change the line spacing of

- a single paragraph?
- the whole document?

How to embolden sections of text?

How to underline sections of text?

How to centre lines?

How to leave a specified vertical space?

How to present a table?

How to number pages in a multi-page document?

As each of these points are needed, you will be told at the beginning of the section, so that you can either learn how to carry out the function or refresh your memory if necessary. The Know Your Display section is there to help you.

KNOW YOUR DISPLAY

ABBREVIATIONS

All abbreviations should be typed out in full unless they are on the list of recognised abbreviations. The following are some examples of the recognised abbreviations.

Example

NB, etc, eg, ie, & (in a company name only), Dr (Doctor).

ALLOCATING SPACE

When allocating space for a given measurement, check to see how many lines the program is currently giving to 1''. Six lines per inch is the normal size, but with different sized fonts in use, this can vary.

REMEMBER - for example to leave 1", the actual space left from the bottom of the last line of type to the next line of type *must not be less than 1''.* It can be greater, but not unreasonably greater - one or two extra line spaces, but no more.

CENTRING

This is carried out automatically by most word processing programs and this facility should always be used to ensure accuracy. Some programs require each line to be centred, but there are some programs which will centre a group of lines with perhaps one or two commands.

A piece of text which has been centred is normally positioned *exactly* in the middle of the space between the left and the right margin.

DATA ENTRY ERRORS

The maximum number of data entry errors allowed is three. Repeated errors count once only.

EMBOLDENING

To embolden means to emphasize specific words or lines. The emboldening may not show on the screen, as it is a printer command, and will show on the final printout in one of two ways:

- the letter is printed once, and then a second time directly on top of the first;

- the letter is printed once, and then a second time fractionally to the right - known as 'shadow printing'.

LINE LENGTH

The document to be keyed in requires a specified line length. At the present time, this is stated as 65 characters, with a plus or minus of three spaces. However, this is virtually impossible to achieve if using proportional spacing. An amended assignment could be used to solve this problem.

LINE SPACING

Block Paragraphs - Single line spacing

No blank lines within the paragraph, but there must be *one* clear line space between paragraphs as in the example below.

```
This short paragraph shows the effect of
leaving an extra line space between blocked
paragraphs in single line spacing.

If a clear line space is not left, the distinc-
tion between the paragraphs is not clear.
```

Block Paragraphs - Double line spacing

One line space between each line within the paragraph, but there must be at least *two* clear spaces between the paragraphs as shown in the following example.

```
This short paragraph shows the effect of

leaving an extra line space between blocked

paragraphs in double line spacing.


If an extra clear line space is not left, the

distinction between the paragraphs is not

obvious.
```

Block Paragraphs - Mixture of double and single line spacing

This causes a great deal of confusion. As a general rule, if only one paragraph is being inserted in double line spacing, one double space either side gives sufficient distinction.

> **This is a sample of a document keyed in single line spacing, with one paragraph in the middle of the document in double line spacing.**
>
> **Before starting the paragraph in double line spacing, leave one double space, and at the end of the paragraph, leave one double space.**
>
> **It is important that the spacing BEFORE and AFTER the double spaced section is the same.**

If more than one paragraph is to be put into double line spacing, there must be a distinction between the paragraphs - normally an extra single or double space.

> **This is a sample of a document keyed in single line spacing, with two paragraphs in the middle of the document in double line spacing.**
>
> **Before starting the paragraph in double line spacing, leave one double space plus an extra space, and at the end of the paragraph, leave a double space plus an extra space.**
>
> **It is essential that there is a distinction between the paragraphs and that the spacing is CONSISTENT. If in doubt, leave an extra space.**
>
> **It is important that the spacing BEFORE and AFTER the double spaced section is the same.**

Remember: Do not use a return at the end of a line to form double line spacing - *change the spacing using the program facility.*

LISTS OF ITEMS

If a list of items is required, the list is usually prefaced by a hyphen or a bullet. The hyphen/bullet is normally placed at the left margin and two or three spaces before the text is typed. If using proportional spacing, it may be necessary to set a tab stop for the text to ensure alignment.

Use single or double line spacing, according to instructions, but never double double line spacing.

MARGINS

Top/Bottom

These two margins are usually determined when the word processing package is installed. Sometimes they can be changed within the document if necessary.

Left/Right

The left and right margins of text are either predetermined on installation, or if they are likely to change with every document, they can be set as desired.
See Line Length.

There are two types of right margin:

Justified right margin

With a justified right margin, the text stops at exactly the same place on the line and gives the document a box-like appearance. This is achieved either by spaces being added between the words, or by adjusting the characters on the line giving equal spaces on either side of the words. The left margin must be justified with 100 per cent consistency throughout the document - any deviation will be penalised.

Ragged right margin

A ragged right margin is of irregular appearance with equal spaces between words.

NUMBERING PAGES

Each page in a multi-page document should be numbered. This can be done, either by using the automatic page numbering facility provided by the program, or by using a header/footer.

The normal position is in the centre of the text in the bottom margin. It is acceptable in any position in either the top or bottom margin - but each page must be numbered in the *same* position.

NUMBERED PARAGRAPHS

There are a variety of ways of producing numbered paragraphs. Use the method which allows the use of wordwrap. Do not use a return at the end of each line, because corrections will be difficult to make, and the justified right margin will be difficult to attain.

Some programs have an automatic paragraph numbering facility.

The following is an example of numbered paragraphs:

```
1       The number is placed at the left margin
        and a tab stop is then pressed to take the
        cursor two or three spaces in before the
        paragraph is keyed in.

2       When the first paragraph has been typed,
        the paragraph should be in a straight
        line, with the numbers only showing at
        the left margin.
```

OPEN PUNCTUATION

It is common practice today to omit all unnecessary punctuation. This does not include the punctuation required for grammatical purposes.

In open punctuation, there are no full stops within:

- the name and address on a letter
- a date
- a reference
- abbreviations eg Mr Mrs NB etc MP BSc

PAGE BREAKS

If asked to force a page break at a specified point, use the facility provided by the program - *do not use returns until the page is completed.*

PARAGRAPHS

There are three basic types of paragraph as shown below:

Block - all lines start at the left margin.

```
This is a sample of a block paragraph. All the
lines start at the left margin, and it is very
easy to display.

The second paragraph would therefore look like
this. Note how easy it is to see the distinction
between the paragraphs.
```

Indented - the first line of *every* paragraph starts half an inch from the left margin.

```
        This is a sample of an indented para-
graph.

        Note how the first line starts half an
inch from the left margin (either 5 or 6 spaces
depending upon the type size being used) and all
other lines start at the left margin.
```

Hanging - the first line starts at the left margin and second and subsequent lines start consistently two or three spaces in from the left margin.

```
This is a sample of a hanging paragraph. In this
     type of paragraph, the first line starts at
     the left margin.

All other lines start consistently two or three
     spaces in from the margin.
```

PRINTING MULTI-PAGE DOCUMENTS

When printing multi-page documents, care must be taken that the paper is positioned correctly, so that the bottom margin is correct. Poor positioning of the paper can result in too small a space if the specified space comes at the bottom of the page.

Remember - poor positioning of printing can spoil an otherwise well-displayed document.

SPACING AFTER PUNCTUATION

One space after	comma (,)
	semi-colon (;)
Two spaces after	full stop (.)
	question mark (?)
	exclamation mark (!)
	colon (:)
One space before and one space after	dash (-)
One space before and no space after	opening double quotes (“)
	opening brackets (
No space before and one space after	closing double quotes (”)
	closing brackets)
No space before and no space after	hyphen (-)
	apostrophe (’) before “s”.

TABLES

The tables required are usually simple columns (either two, three, four or five) with/without underscored headings.

The simplest procedure to follow is to start at the left margin, tap the longest line in the first column, add three spaces and set a tab stop. Repeat this procedure for each column.

The spaces between the columns can be any number, usually depending on the number and size of the columns, but *they must be equal.*

TYPE SIZES

The most common type sizes are 10 or 12 characters to the inch. Most printers allow the size of the type face to be changed within a document.

Today, a number of programs and printers allow the use of proportional spacing, ie the letters are given the amount of space they require, instead of a standard space. Therefore, it is virtually impossible to set a line length of a specified size when using proportional spacing. Ask your tutor for an amended assignment giving a specified line length which can be set.

UNDERLINING

The text indicated should be underlined - no more and no less.

Example

<u>Sample of Correct Underlining</u>
S<u>ample of Incorrect Underlining </u>

The spaces between the words within a group should also be underlined.

SMALL MANUSCRIPT PASSAGES

This section gives practice in typing small passages from manuscript.

DO YOU KNOW? **How to create a document?**
How to set margins to give specific line lengths?
How to set the line spacing to single and/or double?
How to read manuscript text?
How to edit text as it is keyed-in?
How to proofread a document?
How to save a document?
How to print a document?

INSTRUCTIONS

Tasks 1 – 6

- Set a line length of 65 characters or 6.5 inches if using proportional spacing.
- Single line spacing.
- Proofread the document carefully and correct any errors.
- Save the document. Print one copy.
- Recall each task. Change to double line spacing.
- Save the document. Print one copy.

Task 1

Jersey - The Ideal Holiday Island. (put in caps)

Jersey lies about 100 miles from the south coast of England and is also close to France.

The climate is similar to that of the Mediterranean, and makes a holiday on the island very pleasant. Not only are the beaches attractive, but the countryside is varied and interesting.

The capital, St Helier, is a paradise for the shopaholic with many duty free shops offering bargains in jewellery, perfume, drinks and tobacco.

Task 2

HOLIDAYING ABROAD.

Caravanning is a relatively cheap form of taking a holiday, and today many thousands of ~~enthusiat~~ enthusiasts are taking their caravans abroad.

The main problem faced by drivers abroad for the first time is the prospect of having to drive on the "wrong" side of the road, with a caravan hitched to the back. Add to this, the need to wind your way through a strange dock with busy traffic.

On the plus side, there is all the convenience of taking your home with you.

Cross the Channel on one of the ferries, and the Continent is open to you to roam as you wish.

Task 3

SIERRA GOLF BALLS

Sierra Golf Supplies has introduced a revolutionary new 3-piece golf ball - instead of the traditional 2-piece.

CAD-CAM Computer technology has played a great part in the development of new professional golf balls. The dimple design allows an increase of distances the ball can be played without loss of accuracy. Wind drag has been greatly reduced and the weight has been shifted to the outside of the ball for more spin and bite on the greens.

This new process represents a breakthrough in golf ball performance - keeping the distance qualities while offering good ball control.

Task 4

CAMERA TIPS - WHAT IS RED EYE?

Red eye is a phenomenon which is well-known to photographers. The effect can ruin any picture by turning the eyes of the subject into burning red pits.

The blood vessels in the retina of the eye react~~s~~ to the amount of light before the flash is fired. The greater the light, the smaller the irises will shrink, and the less likely that it can reflect off the retina back into the lens. Taken to its logical conclusion, the argument is that if you have enough light to prevent red eye, you do not need a flash in the first place!

Task 5

DISNEYLAND (centre, embolden)

Disneyland, in Southern California, is rapidly becoming the dream holiday for thousands of British children. The host community of Disneyland is called Anaheim, and is surrounded by beautiful beaches, mountains and deserts. Nearby, there are many attractions such as Knott's Berry Farm with its Ghost Town, Camp Snoopy and great shows.

Within visiting distance, the tou^r^ist will also find the Movieland Wax Museum, the Spruce Goose or the beautiful sea life of Marineland.

Many charities are busy raising money to send disabled children on the holiday of a lifetime.

Task 6

HISTORY MAGAZINE

Subscriptions

Thank you for your annual subscription to the History Magazine. This covers 6 issues sent on a 2-monthly basis. Your address card will be made out as on the envelope - please inform us immediately if this is incorrect.

We hope you will enjoy~~ing~~ reading our new magazine, and will recommend us to all your friends, and to anyone else interested in history. If any of them wd like to see a free copy, do send us their name & address and we will send one.

DISPLAY TECHNIQUES

This section gives practice in using a variety of display techniques.

DO YOU KNOW? **How to embolden blocks of text?**
How to underline blocks of text?
How to centre blocks of text?
How to leave specified line spaces?

INSTRUCTIONS

Tasks 1 – 5

- Create a new document for each task.
- Follow the instructions given within the tasks.
- Save the document. Print one copy.

Task 1

COMPUTERS! COMPUTERS! COMPUTERS!

All famous names

AMSTRAD
APPLE
IBM

Call$ for latest prices!

0221 765926

<u>Operator</u>: Centre all lines - use double line spacing throughout.

Task 2 – Centre each line

SIERRA THEATRE COMPANY (Embolden)

present

BLACK AND WHITE (Embolden)

by

Johnathon McElwee

Thursday, Friday, Saturday (Underscore)

9, 10, 11 May

at

7.30 pm

Prices: £7.50, £10.00, £12.50

↓ Underscore this word only.

Task 3 – Centre each line

ST ANDREWS BOYS' BRIGADE

(Leave 2 clear line spaces)

CAR BOOT SALE (← embolden)

(Leave 2 clear line spaces)

Saturday, 18 July } underscore

Commencing 2 pm }

at

The Black Bull Inn (← change to u.c.)

Lodge Lane

Fee: £2 per car

Task 4 — Centre all lines

SIERRA OFFICE SUPPLIES
172 Alexandria Grove
EASTHAM
EH6 4LM
} Single spacing

SALE NOW ON (embolden)

Computers
Typewriters
Photocopiers
Laser printers
uc/ Fax machines
} Single spacing

Ring now for detail
SALE HOTLINE - 0621 216179 (embolden)
24 hour recorded price list
} double spacing

Task 5 — Centre all lines.

FLICKERS VIDEO LIBRARY (- caps, embolden)
Tel: 07825 73575

25 Church Street, Campbeltown
(Leave 3 clear lines)
SPECIAL OFFERS - (sp caps/emb)
for
great home entertainment
over the holiday
(Leave 3 clear lines)
SPECIAL OFFER TO MEMBERS (caps/emb)
on Friday & Saturday

Take 3 films on 48 hour hire
and receive your 4th film
FREE - (sp. caps/embolden)

COLUMN WORK

This section gives practice in typing columns of text on their own and within blocks of text.

DO YOU KNOW? **How to type text in columns?**
How to ensure that the space between the columns is equal?
How to underscore the headings over columns?
What line spacing to leave above and below columns?

INSTRUCTIONS

Tasks 1 – 6

- Create a new document.
- Leave equal spaces between columns.
- Underscore headings if indicated in text.

Task 1

BULK PRINTING PRICES

Size	25+	50+	100+	500+
Miniprint	.09	.07	.06	.05
4 x 6	.12	.11	.10	.10
6 x 8	.31	.25	.22	.19
8 x 10	.55	.46	.43	.40
8 x 12	.66	.56	.52	.48

Task 2

HOLIDAY INSURANCE – embolden

Premiums	Per Adult	Per Child
Up to 2 nights	£7.50	£3.75
Up to 4 nights	£8.00	£4.00
Up to 9 nights	£8.50	£4.25
Up to 16 nights	£11.00	£5.50

Task 3

SIERRA CAR HIRE – embolden

Group	Make and Model	Per Day	Per Week
A	Tiger 1000	£6.00	£36.00
B	Lion 1400	£9.00	£54.00
C	Lion 1600	£10.00	£60.00
D	Panther 1800	£10.50	£63.00
E	Puma 2000	£14.00	£84.00
F	12 Seater Minibus	£15.50	£93.00

Task 4

BUILDING SOCIETY – embolden

Account Type	Investment Rates	Gross Interest	Net Interest
30 Day Notice	Under £5000	£7.20	£5.40
	£5000 - £9999	£11.69	£8.77
	£10000 - £24999	£12.92	£9.69
	£25000 - up	£13.23	£9.92

Task 5

CARD OF THE COURSE

TOURNAMENT - SEPTEMBER

} Double spacing Emboldened

(Leave 4 clear line spaces)

Hole	Yards	Par	Hole	Yards	Par
1	375	4	10	325	4
2	400	4	11	170	3
3	360	4	12	316	4
4	450	4	13	400	4
5	570	5	14	536	5
6	400	4	15	397	4
7	365	4	16	376	4
8	160	3	17	481	4
9	340	4	18	367	4

Task 6

VISIT THE STATELY HOMES ← Centre Embolden

Many people, both from home and abroad, enjoy visiting the stately homes of England which are to be found throughout the country. The following is a list of some of the places which can be visited - some of them open throughout the year.

Stately Home	Telephone No
Francombe House	(0974) 318621
Pleasey Place	(76215) 23498
Carwood Castle	(0621) 83817
Cranstone Palace	(0917) 73561

For opening hours - ring the numbers given above.

NUMBERED/BULLETED PASSAGES

This section gives practice in typing numbered paragraphs, or paragraphs starting with bullets.

DO YOU KNOW? **How to set the format for this type of paragraph?**
The spacing to leave between the paragraphs?
The line spacing to leave before/after the block of paragraphs?
How to underscore headings?

Tasks 1 – 6

INSTRUCTIONS

- Set margins to give a line length of 65 characters or 6.5 inches if using proportional spacing.
- Use single line spacing.
- Leave a double line space between paragraphs.
- Put the number or the bullet at the left margin.
- Leave either two, three or four spaces, consistently, between the number/bullet and the paragraph.
- Underscore where indicated in the passages.
- Follow the instructions in each passage for underscoring and emboldening.

Task 1

JERSEY - THE FLORAL ISLAND / Centre Embolden

Jersey is an island full of interesting places. The list below gives an idea of some of the variety:

- Jersey Potteries
- Fort Regent - an entertainment centre with shows, cafes, bars, swimming and skating - everything for the family.
- Tropical Gardens
- Butterfly Farm
- German Underground Hospital
- L'Etacq Wood Carvers
- Golf Course

Task 2

GUIDANCE FOR THE USE OF PERSONAL SCALES

1. Weigh yourself on the same scale placed on the same floor surface. Uneven carpets and deep-pile carpets may affect readings.
2. Weigh yourself at the same time each day, before meals. First thing in the morning is a good time.
3. Weigh yourself without clothing, and never wear shoes or boots.
4. Stand upright with your feet equally spaced on the scale platform and remain as still as possible until the display settles.

Task 3

Scented Beauty

1. Keep scented flowers away from a dinner table. They can be too overpowering mixed with appetising food smells and the delicate aroma of wines.
2. Likewise, heavily scented flowers can prove too strong in a bedroom.
3. Ideal sites for strongly scented flowers are halls, where the perfume greets you and wafts through into the other rooms or sitting rooms.
4. My favourites include lily of the valley, hyacinth, narcissus, gardenia, stock and tobacco plants. This last one is most fragrant at night.

DO YOU KNOW? How to type sums of money in text?

How to type brackets around words/groups of words?

Task 4

COVER AND LIMITS → Centre heading

1. Personal accidents up to £10.000.
2. Medical expenses up to £100,000.
3. Loss of deposit or cancellation up to £1,500.
4. Delayed departure benefit up to £20 for the first full 12 hours and £10 for each subsequent full 12 hours, maximum £60.
5. Missed departure due to failure of public transport (outward journey only) up to £300.
6. Loss of personal baggage up to £1,000.
7. Personal money (actual cash £250) up to £350.
8. Personal liability up to £500,000.
9. 24 hour emergency assistance.

Task 5

GARDENING JOBS

It is essential that all the jobs which need to be carried out in the garden are done in the right month.

July

- Spray roses regularly.
- Trim back long shoots on spring-flowering rockery plants.
- Check plants have sufficient water in pots/containers.
- Feed plants in pots/containers regularly.
- Move ferns from hot sunny windows.
- Sow lettuce, rad~~d~~ish, beetroots and carrots for late cropping.
- Remove side-shoots of greenhouse tomatoes.

Task 6

AGENDA (sp caps/embolden)

The AGM of the Dexter Sports & Social Club is to be held on 14th January at 6.30 pm at the Club Room.

1 Apologies for absence
2 Minutes of last meeting
3 Matters arising
4 Correspondence
5 Officer(s) Reports
6. New premises
7 Annual Games Programme
8 Any other business
9 Date of next meeting

Double line spacing

ALLOCATION OF VERTICAL SPACE

This section gives practice in allocating vertical space of a specified size.

DO YOU KNOW? **How many line spaces there are to 1"?**
How to leave space of a specified size?
How to underscore headings?
How to centre headings?
How to embolden headings?

INSTRUCTIONS

Tasks 1 – 5

Create a new document.

Follow the individual task instructions for the size of space to be left.

Follow the individual task instructions for underscoring, centring and emboldening.

Follow the layout of each task for use of capitals, lower case, etc.

Save each copy.

Print one copy of each task.

Task 1

YOUR DUTY AS A DOG OWNER

Training

A well-trained dog is a much happier pet than an untrained one. If you take a little time and trouble you will find that the companionship of an obedient dog more than repays your effort.

(leave a 1" space)

When to Start Training

Start training your ~~pet~~ dog when he is still a puppy and then, at around 6 months, and when vaccinations have been completed, enrol him in a local dog training class.

(leave a 2" space)

Why Train?

A puppy has natural instincts which do not conform to the domestic requirements of his owner. Like any youngster, he needs to be taught that there is a right and wrong way to behave.

(leave a 1½" space)

Look after your dog and he will look after you.

Task 2

Centre Embolden

THE TREASURE HOUSES OF ENGLAND

England has a large number of beautiful old houses which can be visited by the holiday maker.

Woburn Abbey

Woburn Abbey has been in the family of the Dukes of Bedford for over 300 years. The park surrounding Woburn Abbey has a magnificent herd of deer consisting of 9 different species. Banqueting and conference facilities are available throughout the year

(Leave 1" space)

Warwick Castle

Warwick Castle contains a magnificent collection of arms and armour used down through the centuries. There are peacocks roaming in the delightful gardens which were designed by Capability Brown.

(Leave 1" space)

Chatsworth House

Chatsworth, built between 1686 and 1708, is the home of the Duke and Duchess of Devonshire. A route is clearly marked through the house for visitors to follow at their leisure. The gardens are spectacular.

(Leave 1" space)

A visit to these storehouses of the history of our land is really well worth while.

Task 3

SUPPORTING A DAMAGED FENCE POST

Rotten fence posts are a problem for the gardener, particularly if the fence is a long one. The remedy could be costly and involve taking down the whole fence. There is, however, a less costly solution, and that is to use a concrete spur. When finished, the spur can be stained to the colour of the fence to make it less conspicuous.

<u>Steps</u>

Clear the ground around the damaged post.

Leave 1"

Dig a hole at least 2' deep, keeping the sides as vertical as possible, and remove the rotted section of the post.

Leave 1"

Anchor the post, insert the spur and mark and drill the holes in the post for the bolts.

Leave 1"

Place rubble around the spur and fill with quick-setting concrete, flattening well.

Leave 1"

Insert the bolts and washers and tighten well.

Leave 1"

Stain the concrete to blend with the rest of the fence.

Task 4

ATTENTION (– sp caps/centre)

Following these few basic operating tips will greatly enhance the performance of your new shredder by reducing the risk of damage and/or operating problems.

1. Read operating instructions carefully before using.
2. If machine was exposed to cold weather, allow to warm to room temperature before using.
3. To avoid jamming and ensure complete shredding – do not feed paper wider than throat – do not exceed recommended sheet capacity – always feed paper squarely into machine.

Leave 2"

4. Do not allow paper clips to be fed into machine – always remove.

Leave 2"

5. Unplug power jack from machine when emptying waste receptacle.

Leave 2"

6. When emptying waste receptacle, remove any paper build up from underside of machine.

Task 5

OPERATOR: Use double spacing.

ADJUSTING A BALL VALVE

There are a number of methods of adjusting a ball valve according to the type of valve involved. The following are some ideas you may like to follow:

If the valve is one of the modern diaphragm type, all that may be necessary is to move the float up and down on the serrated spindle which is connected to the valve arm.

(Leave 1½")

If the valve is one of the modern type which have a small adjusting screw close to the valve mechanism, it is necessary to screw it further in to lower the water level, or out to raise the water level.

(Leave 1½")

Adjust the older type of Portsmouth valve by carefully bending the ball arm. Never hold the ball while bending, as it may break off from the arm.

(Leave 1½") Operator: Start a new page here if insuff sp

If there is a damaged ball of an older pattern, this can be unscrewed and replaced.

(Leave 1½").

MULTI-PAGE DOCUMENTS

This section gives practice in typing and setting out multi-page documents.

DO YOU KNOW? **How to 'break' a page at a sensible point?**
What a 'widow' is?
What an 'orphan' is?
How to start a new page at a given point?
How to number the pages?
Where to number the pages?
How to print a multi-page document?

All tasks

INSTRUCTIONS

- Set margins to a line length of 65 characters or to 6.5 inches if using proportional spacing.
- Use single or double line spacing as indicated within each task.
- Number each page.
- Where there are tabulated sections, display them with equal spaces between the columns.
- Use the display already used for numbered/bulleted items in the earlier section.
- Save the documents and print one copy of each.

Task 1

TYPIST: Put the first paragraph in double line spacing and the remainder in single line spacing.

GARDEN SAFETY FOR PETS – Centre/Emb.

In the summer, many people spend more time in the garden. This also appeals to our pets who enjoy lazing in the shade. The garden can be a dangerous place for humans, but more especially for pets.

CHEMICALS – (for all side headings, use l.c and u.s.)

Chemicals may need to be used on the lawns to kill moss, or on the roses to kill greenfly. If this is so, pets could get this on to their fur and lick it off, thus poisoning themselves.

Read all instructions carefully, and spray when pets are not around.

(Leave 1")

CREOSOTE

Make sure the creosoted surfaces are dry before allowing pets into the treated area. Store all brushes and containers out of harm's way.

(Leave 1")

SLUG PELLETS

Some slug pellets have a bran base which pets will find tasty, but will have disastrous consequences if

eaten. There are a wide range of pellets available, so choose one which is not harmful to pets if you have any.
(leave 1")
POWER TOOLS
The tools used in the garden today are, increasingly, electrically powered. This long line of cable creeping across the lawn could appear to a pet to be an ideal plaything. If your pet has a tendency to chew or to chase things, keep them safe indoors while using equipment they are likely to play with.
(leave 1")
LITTER
Dispose of all litter immediately to avoid potential harm by plastic bags or cans.

Task 2 (leave 2")

TYPIST: Use single line spacing for main text, but double spacing for numbered items.

Date as Postmark (caps)
Dear Customer
SERVICING OF SOLID FUEL APPLIANCES
You will be very pleased to learn that I have been able to make special arrangements for you to have your solid fuel appliance serviced by experts. This means that you can be

sure you are getting the best, most econo-
mical use out of your heating system.

Regular maintenance means safety too,
and a correctly serviced appliance will
give years of trouble-free operation.
This scheme is only available to selected
solid fuel users and I have been able
to arrange this for my customers. The
scheme is available from 1st July to
30th September and details are as
follows:

1. Sweep chimney.
2. Check and adjust fit of firebars.
3. Check and adjust carriage frame
and ashpit cover.
4. Check and adjust thermostat assembly
(roomheaters and boilers).
5. Check and clear flueways and flue
plate.
6. Check and clear damper assembly.
7 Replace (as necessary) firebars, fire-
bricks, asbestos seals, fire cement
joints.

The charge for these services will be
£35 for open fires, and £45 for all
other appliances (prices include VAT).

The cost of any replacement parts is not included in the service but will be charged as an extra.

I am sure you will want to take advantage of this scheme so that you can confidently face next winter. Remember last winter and you will realise how important it is to keep your heating system in good condition.

Thank you for your valued custom and I enclose a pre-paid postcard which you should complete and return so that arrangements can be made for your appliance to be serviced.

Yours sincerely

Coal Merchant

Enc.

Task 3

Recall the document for Task 2 - change numbered items to single line spacing and remainder to double line spacing. Add the following before Enc.

PS Send in your card as soon as poss to ensure prompt attention indicating the most suitable period for the service.

Task 4

MOBILE HAIRDRESSING

(TYPIST: Use double line spacing.

A new branch of hairdressing has grown up over the last four or five years, and that is 'mobile' hairdressing. Instead of having fixed premises and set opening hours, the mobile hairdresser works in the home of his/her clients, visiting at times convenient to both.

This is a very useful for the frail, infirm housebound person - They can still have the latest styles while not moving from their home.

There are also advantages for the hair-dressers. They do not have the expense of running a salon, with water, electricity, heating, and local tax payments as well as the expensive fixtures and fittings. Working in the comfort of the clients' homes, they use their water and electricity. The only expense they have is the car or van which provides them with their mobility, and the various rollers, curlers, hairdryers and blowers, and lotions which they carry with them.

The following is an example price list sent to homes by a mobile hairdresser in my area.

Acid wave	£25.00
Cold wave	£15 - £20.00
Cut and Blow	£7.00
Cut and Blow Gents	£5.50
Children up to	£6.00
Cut only	£3.00
Blow wave	£4.50
High Lights	£16.00
Tint	£12.50
Tint and Cut	£16.00

Use single line spacing

The following special offer was also included with the Price List.

PRESENT THIS TICKET AND YOU CAN HAVE £3.00 off Acid Wave or £1.00 off any price (TYPIST: All this shd be in caps).

A leaflet was attached giving examples of different kinds of hair styles as follows:

Example Style

Leave 1½"

Mobile hairdressers are providing a good service to the housebound population.

Task 5

DRYING FLOWERS

Use single spacing

It used to take weeks to dry flowers, but now you will have them in no time at all.

Some flowers lend themselves perfectly to drying while others may change colour or fade. Do not be afraid to experiment. The following information is meant to serve as a guide to get you started.

It is a good idea to start with flowers of a lighter colour because most flowers tend to darken during drying. Brightly coloured flowers such as roses, daffodils, daisies and carnations work best. Yellow flowers retain their colour especially well. Thick flowers such as iris or saucer magnolia do not dry well. White flowers tend to become dull gray-brown.

Cut flowers that are cool and dry, usually in the early morning, late afternoon or evening. Do not cut flowers that are wet with rain or dew. The flowers should be about half open and firm. Flowers in full bloom may lose their petals when dried. Dry flowers as soon as possible after cutting, to preserve their colour. If you cannot dry them when first cut, store flowers in a refrigerator or a cool place until you are ready.

Preparing the Flowers

Pour silica gel into the container to a depth of about two inches.

Leave 1½"

Cut flower stems to a length of one inch.

Leave 1"

Insert flowers right side up, spacing them so that they do not touch each other or the container sides. Use a toothpick to separate the petals and to help petals retain their original shape.

Leave 1"

Gently sift silica gel over the flowers until covered, working it up and around so that the silica gel is in contact with all flower parts. Gently tapping the container helps the grain fill in around the petals.

Leave 1"

<u>Drying the Flowers</u>

Place container of flowers in the microwave with a cup of water. Use high (100%) power according to time chart. Because microwaves act quickly on the flowers, more colour is retained than when the flowers are air dried or dried for many days in silica gel only. Using the water in the microwave keeps the flowers from becoming brittle.

Leave 1"

After heating for the specified time, it helps to leave the container undisturbed in the micro-wave overnight. If desired, you may carefully remove the container and cover with foil. But moving may dislodge silica gel crystals around the flowers which may affect their final colour.

Leave 1½"

Test for Dryness. Before removing flowers, gently move away enough silica gel to touch the petals. If they do not seem completely dry, you may wish to re^cover the flower and return the container to the microwave for one minute. All flowers dry somewhat differently.

(Start new page here)

Drying Tip

If the blue crystals in the silica gel begin to turn pink, the gel is losing its capability to absorb the moisture. To reconstitute the gel, just heat in the microwave for a few minutes until the blue colour returns. By doing this, you can use the same silica gel over and over again for several years.

Removing the Flowers

Tip the container gently so the silica gel crystals begin to slowly flow off the flowers. As flowers become exposed, carefully slide two fingers under the flower to remove. Gently shake off excess crystals.

Leave 1½"

Place flowers in a 'dry box' for three to five days for longer lasting dry flowers. Use a metal or plastic container. Add silica gel to a depth of about one inch. Insert flowers so just the stems are in the silica gel. Cover with a tight fitting lid.

Leave 1½"

If you are not going to use the flowers immediately, storing them in a box of shredded newspapers or tissue papers will

help them hold their shape until needed. Keep them in a dry place. Adding a teaspoon of silica gel in the container corners helps keep flowers dry.
Leave 1½"
Use a fine soft brush to carefully dust off any remaining crystals.

Task 6

SIGMA MICROWAVES

The Browning Element

} centre/embolden

The browner in your microwave oven gives food a light golden-brown 'finished' look, and adds a little extra crispness to foods.

The browning element will glow red in about 90 seconds after it is turned on. This has been taken into consideration in the browning times suggested. The browning then may require from 5 to 13 minutes to achieve the browning and crisping desired. The microwave oven door must be closed for the browning element to operate. Every time the door is opened, the element turns off, and begins to cool. Thus, opening the door to check foods may prolong the suggested browning times.

(Operator - type the next paragraph only in double line spacing.)

It is not necessary to change rack

positions during the entire cooking and browning operation. The glass tray shelf has been designed to be used as a cooking utensil.

(Start new page)

<u>To use the Browner</u>

1. Place food directly under the browning element in the rack position desired. Close the door.

2. Push the 'Brown' button (or pad, on touch control models).

(Leave 1½")

3. Push the 'Start' button (or pad, on the touch models). The 'Brown' indicator light will come on, and the element will heat. The element will shut off automatically when the time set has elapsed.

4. Push 'Off' button to shut off the interior light and stirrer. (If you open the door during browning, you will need to press the 'Start' button (or pad) to continue the browning operation).

<u>Suggested Cooking Times</u>

The following is a brief idea of the cooking times for different kinds of food, together with the browning times. It is important to remember that the cooking times vary according to the power output of the microwave, but the browning times should be accurate.

Dish	Cooking Time	Browning Time
Chicken & Rice Casserole	20	30
Chicken Pieces	10	10
El Paso Casserole	10	8
Lamb Chops	22	7
Sausage Patties	5	8
Hamburger Palties	3	8

Hints and Tips

Do not use a dinner plate or any plastic or paper products. They could crack, char, melt or catch fire. Always use a microwave ovenproof glass or ceramic dish that will withstand the heat from the browning element.

Use potholders when removing food from under the browner. Remember the dishes will be hot.

The probe should never be used with the browning element. Always remove it before the element is turned on.

Do not touch the browning element when it is hot, you could get burned.

If foods have spattered on the element, it will burn itself clean during the first part of the browning operation.

(Leave 1")

Use your browner correctly. — Centre, emb, in caps.

Task 7

SIERRA SUPER VIDEO CASSETTE (with "S" inserted)

HOW TO USE AND STORE

Precautions for use -(emb/us)

(Lines 1–3: centre)

Make sure that the cassette is inserted into the recorder in the correct way.

(Leave 2")

The tape will play from left to right and then end. Before use, check that the round tape window on the left of the cassette is full. If not, rewind the tape before using. Whenever possible load and unload tapes which have been completely unwound. Avoid unnecessary insertion and ejection of the cassette while the tape is stopped midway, as this may create slackening of the tape resulting in damage or breakage.

Disassembling the cassette for any reason, or splicing the tape is not advised. It may cause permanent damage.

Handle the cassette carefully. AVOID sudden shocks such as dropping the cassette.

(Start new page)

To Prevent Accidental Erasure

/ (Type the following in double line spacing)

Accidental erasure of an important recording can be prevented by simply removing the tab at the side of the cassette. Re-recording can be accomplished by affixing a piece of adhesive tape over the opening created by the removal of the tab.

(Leave 2")

Precautions for Proper Storage

1. Make sure that the tape is evenly wound before storage. If the wind is uneven, the tape should be rewound a second time.
2. Always place the cassette in its cover case and store in a vertical position.
3. Avoid dusty or dirty places
4. Prolonged exposure to moisture can damage the tape. Keep the cassettes away from humidity.
5. DO NOT place cassettes in an area where they will be exposed to direct sunlight or heat from appliances.
6. DO NOT place cassettes on a car dashboard or on the rear window shelf of the car.
7. Keep cassettes away from strong magnetic fields (motors, transformers, magnets etc)

Look after your cassettes and they will give you many hours of pleasure.

Task 8

INSTRUCTIONS – Type the text in the numbered paras in single line spacing, and the remainder in double line spacing.

LOADING FILM ~~IN YOUR CAMERA~~ (centre/Emb)

The loading of the film on the spiral has, so far, not been considered in any detail. The loading procedure does, of course, depend on the type of spiral being used. The <u>self-loading</u> spiral is widely used, and this type of spiral will be considered first. Self-loading spirals have rotating flanges and a gripping device on the outermost groove which allows the film to pass through in one direction only. Rotating the flanges backwards and forwards by a small amount causes the film to be drawn into the spiral.

The procedure for self-loading spirals is as follows:

1. Make sure that the openings on both flanges of the spiral are opposite one another and insert the film into the grooves with its emulsion side towards the centre of the spiral.
2. To aid the introduction of the film into the spiral, grip the end of the film and pull it into the spiral for several inches, to ensure that it is brought past the one-way gripping device.
3. Hold the spiral with both hands, so that one thumb is near each groove entrance.
4. Place one thumb on the edge of the film and rotate the flanges against one another.

The pressure of your thumb on the film will stop the film coming out of the spiral.

5. Reverse the procedure by applying pressure with your other thumb and rotate the flanges in opposite directions. Repeating the oscillating movement of the flanges causes the film to be drawn into the grooves.

6. When the film is fully loaded, cut or tear the film from the backing paper or film spool.

7. Place the spiral in the tank and put the lid on firmly.

Some people prefer the centre-loading type of spiral in which the film is loaded from the centre outwards after clipping the film to the central core. Because 35 mm films are narrower than other roll films, they are easier to use in these spirals. [The procedure for centre-loading spirals is as follows:

1. While holding the spiral in one hand, curve the film by pressing the edges toward one another with thumb and index finger of your other hand. The film will just clear the grooves.

2. Insert the curved film in the spiral and fasten it to the clip on the central core.

3. Rotate the spiral while gently feeding in the curved film. As the film moves across the grooves and the pressure which holds it curved is released, it drops into the correct groove. Do not allow a groove to be missed or the film may buckle and stick to the neighbouring ~~row~~ turn, resulting in an uneven circulation of processing solutions.

4. Cut the film from the spool or backing paper and place it in the developing tank.

UNIT 4

GRAPHICAL REPRESENTATION OF NUMERICAL DATA

For this unit you will need to know how to extract data from source documents and present it in a graphical format.

DO YOU KNOW ?

How to draw a pie chart?

How to draw a line graph?

How to draw a histogram?

How to extract the relevant figures from source documents?

How to decide which type of graph to use?

How to enter the correct data?

How to label the graph clearly?

How to print the graph?

How to save the data to be recalled at a later date?

As each of these points are needed, you will be told at the beginning of the section, so that you can either learn how to carry out the function or refresh your memory.

HINTS AND TIPS

1 Check carefully that only the relevant figures are extracted from the data.

2 Check carefully that only the correct figures are entered.

3 When labels are entered, they must be clear and presented either in full, or appropriately abbreviated - note the word *appropriately. Do not allow* the text to overflow so that it becomes unreadable.

4 Proofread *all text carefully* - no more than three data entry errors are allowed.

5 Choose the type of graph which will show clearly the differences in the extracted data.

6 Choose the type of graph which will print clearly.

ASSIGNMENT 1

For this set of tasks you will need Source Documents A for Sierra Car Hire (pages 98 - 102.

DO YOU KNOW? **How to extract data from source documents?**
How to enter the data?
How to draw a pie chart?
How to add headings and subheadings to a pie chart?
How to label a pie chart?
How to save a pie chart?
How to print a pie chart?

Task 1

Hirers can take out an additional insurance premium if they wish. Extract the figures for those hirers who have taken out insurance and those who have not. Present the information in the form of a pie chart. Use the following headings and labels:

Main Heading: SIERRA CAR HIRE

Subheading: INSURANCE PREMIUMS

Labels: YES or NO.

Save the graph and print one copy.

Task 2

The hirers of the cars have the choice of picking up their vehicles from the airport, the harbour or the hotel. Extract the figures for each picking up point and display the figures in the form of a pie chart. Use the following headings and labels:

Main Heading: SIERRA CAR HIRE

Subheading: PICK UP POINTS

Labels: Use appropriate labels

Save the graph and print one copy.

Task 3

The hirers of the cars also have the choice of dropping off their vehicles at the airport, the harbour or the hotel. They do not necessarily drop off at the same point as they pick up. Your employer wants a graph to compare with that for Task 2 to show how many hirers use the different drop off points. Extract the figures for the dropping off points and present the figures in the form of a pie chart. Use the following headings and labels:

Main Heading: SIERRA CAR HIRE

Subheading: DROP OFF POINTS

Labels: Use an appropriate label for each segment.

Save the graph and print one copy.

Task 4

The cars hired are all in the Excelsior range of models. Extract the figures for each model of car hired and present the figures in the form of a pie chart. Use the following heading and labels:

Heading: MODELS HIRED

Labels: Use the name of the model of the car

Save the graph and print one copy.

DO YOU KNOW? **How to produce a histogram?**
How to add headings and subheadings to a histogram?
How to label a histogram?

Task 5

In Tasks 2 and 3 data was selected to produce pie charts to show the picking up and the dropping off points of hired cars. Your employer has decided that the pie charts do not show the data to the best advantage. Using the figures extracted from Tasks 2 and 3 re-present the data in the form of a histogram. Use the following heading and labels:

Heading: PICK UP AND DROP OFF POINTS

Labels: Use appropriate labels or abbreviations.

Save and print one copy of the graph.

DO YOU KNOW? **How to produce a line graph?**
How to add headings and subheadings to a line graph?
How to label a line graph?

Task 6

Your employer would like to see which of the groups of car are most popular for hiring. There are five groups of car on hire. Extract the figures for each group and present them in the form of a line graph. Use the following headings and labels:

Main Heading: SIERRA CAR HIRE

Subheading: GROUPS OF CAR HIRED

Labels: Use appropriate labels.

Save and print one copy of the graph.

ASSIGNMENT 2

For this set of tasks you will need Source Documents B for Sierra Theatre Bookings (pages 103 - 7).

Task 1

Sierra Theatre Bookings book tickets for shows throughout the North West of England. Extract the figures for each of the towns indicated on the booking forms and present the figures in the form of a pie chart. Use the following heading and labels:

Heading: SHOW TOWNS

Labels: Use the names of the towns, or if these will not fit use a recognised abbreviation.

Save and print one copy of the graph.

Task 2

Using the figures extracted for the pie chart for Task 1, re-present the information in the form of a histogram. Use the same heading and labels.

Save and print one copy of the revised graph.

Task 3

Using the figures extracted for the pie chart for Task 1, re-present the information in the form of a line graph. Use the same heading and labels.

Save and print one copy of the revised graph.

DO YOU KNOW? How to explode a segment in a pie chart?

Task 4

Sierra Theatre Bookings offer three alternative methods of payment - cash, cheque or credit card. The management is reviewing the methods and has asked you to present the figures to show which is the most popular method of payment. Extract the figures and present them in the form of a pie chart - exploding the segment for the method most commonly used. Use the following heading and labels:

Heading: METHODS OF PAYMENT

Labels: Cheque, Credit Card, Cash - or recognised abbreviations.

Save and print one copy of the graph.

Task 5

The seats booked are for the stalls, the circle and the balcony. Extract the figures for each and present them in the form of a line graph. Use the following headings and labels:

Heading: SEAT BOOKINGS

Labels: Stalls, Circle, Balcony.

Save and print one copy of the graph.

Task 6

Sierra are currently booking for four shows in the North West. Extract the figures for the shows from the booking forms and present them in the form of a histogram. Use the following heading and labels:

Heading: SHOWS

Labels: Use appropriate labels.

Save and print one copy of the graph.

ASSIGNMENT 3

For this set of tasks you will need Source Documents C for Sierra Property Company (pages 108 - 17).

DO YOU REMEMBER?	**How to extract data from source documents?**
	How to draw a line chart?
	How to draw a histogram?
	How to draw a pie chart?
	How to save the chart?
	How to print the chart?

Task 1

The questionnaire completed by clients asks them to indicate whether or not they are first time buyers. Using the questionnaires extract the numbers who indicated that they are first time buyers and those who are not. Draw a pie chart to show the figures for *yes* and for *no*. Label the chart sensibly.

Save the graph and print one copy.

Task 2

The questionnaires also show the numbers of clients who wish to have mortgage facilities provided. Extract the figures for those who do and those who do not. Draw a pie chart to show the figures for *yes* and *no*. Label the chart sensibly.

Save the graph and print one copy.

Task 3

Using the questionnaires, extract the figures for those people who have a property for sale and those who do not. Draw a pie chart to represent the figures. Use appropriate headings and labels for the chart.

Save the graph and print one copy.

Task 4

The questionnaire completed by clients asks for information on the current property of the client. Using that section of the form, extract the data for the types of gardens attached to the properties. The information given is either *none, small* or *large*. Extract the relevant figures under each heading and prepare a pie chart to illustrate those figures. Use the main heading SIERRA PROPERTIES, subheading GARDENS and segment labels NONE, SMALL and LARGE.

Save the graph and print one copy.

Task 5

As sales clerk at the Sierra Property Company, one of your weekly tasks is to analyse the types of property which are required by customers. Extract the numbers of each of the seven types of property which have been requested, and prepare the data in the form of a histogram. Use the abbreviations given in Database Assignment 3 for the property types. Use a main heading SIERRA PROPERTIES and a subheading PROPERTIES FOR PURCHASE. The axis labels should be the same as the abbreviations.

Save the graph and print one copy.

Task 6

Prospective purchasers have been asked to indicate their requirements for gardens using the general headings - small, large or none. Analyse the data given and prepare a pie chart to illustrate the figures. Use an appropriate heading and labels.

Save the chart and print one copy.

Task 7

For the weekly partners' meeting you have been asked to provide data on the number of reception rooms which are required by clients. This is to be part of a nationwide survey undertaken by the group to which your organisation belongs. Each branch is requested to produce the information in the form of a pie chart.

The main heading is to be SIERRA PROPERTIES, with a subheading RECEPTION ROOMS. Use the numbers as the segment labels.

Save the pie chart and print two copies, one of which will be used in the report to be sent to Head Office at the end of each week for the next month.

Task 8

Your organisation serves the County, and for the weekly partners' meeting you have been asked to give an indication of the towns in which clients currently reside. Look at the forms completed by the clients during the past week and extract the names of the towns and the numbers of properties within each town. Prepare the data for presentation in the form of a histogram. Use appropriate main headings and axis headings.

Save the graph and print two copies.

Task 9

There is a partners' meeting each week and they require different types of graph to illustrate the local trends. They have asked you to look at the documents which clients have completed and extract the statistics for the numbers of bedrooms which are required for all types of property. Extract the relevant figures and prepare them in the form of a line graph. Use appropriate main headings and axis headings.

Save the graph and print two copies.

Task 10

For the weekly report to Head Office mentioned in Task 6, you also need to produce a chart indicating the types of property to be sold. Look at the details on the forms completed by the clients for houses to be sold and extract the number of each type of property. Prepare the details in the form of a pie chart ready for inclusion in that report.

Use the main heading SIERRA PROPERTIES, the subheading HOUSES TO BE SOLD, and use the numbers for the segment labels.

Save the chart and print two copies. One of these copies is to be used in the report to be sent to Head Office.

Task 11

Using the data extracted for Task 5, ie the types of properties to be purchased, and that for Task 10, ie the types of properties to be sold, prepare a comparative line chart or histogram to show the differences. Use appropriate headings and labels.

Save the graph and print two copies.

UNIT 5

COLLATING INFORMATION

For this unit, you will need to know how to extract data from spreadsheets and databases, and to add these and a graph to a word processed document.

DO YOU KNOW ?

How to extract the correct information from the database, spreadsheet and word processed document, including relevant headings?

How to insert the extract into the correct position using either 'cut and paste' or desktop publishing or an integrated package?

How to make sure that the space before/after the extract is sufficient but not excessive?

How to repaginate the word processed document to take account of inserts?

How to mark the presence of an appendix?

How to produce the final document in a manner which is acceptable?

As each of these points are needed, you will be told at the beginning of the passage, so that you can either learn how to carry out the function or refresh your memory.

HINTS AND TIPS

1 If you are using 'cut and paste' always make two copies of your word processed document and the extracts which are required. *Do not use* the original documents for the collated document.

2 If you are using an integrated package or desktop publishing, always provide original printouts plus the collated document.

3 Include the same extract in the collated document as in the original extract.

4 Remember to repaginate the document if the graph is to be added as an appendix.

5 Indicate the inclusion of the graph as an appendix in the appropriate place, in an appropriate manner.

Task 1a

Type one copy of the following document. Use justified right margin, double line spacing and a line length of 65 or 6.5". Number the pages. Save and print.

CAR HIRE Centre and embolden

This Company has chosen to use the Excelsior range as one of the range of models for its car hire service. They have proved very popular with all hirers, because of the range offered. The following graph shows the numbers of the different models hired.

Start new page here.

It is not always easy to offer a full range of cars of the same manufacture, which give the consistency of quality provided by the Excelsior.

The breakdown record has been good, with only 5 cars giving hirers any problems over the past 6 months. The after sales service provided by the manufacturer resulted in these 5 hirers being inconvenienced for a maximum of only 4 hours. This is a considerably better record than with the previous range used.

Task 1b

Recall the document created for Task 1a and insert the graph from page 79 Task 4 at the end of the first page. Either use a printout of the graph to create Appendix A or use the copy saved from your integrated package. Remember to make the relevant amendment to the word processed document if you have created Appendix A. Repaginate the document if necessary.

Task 2a

Type one copy of the following document. Use single line spacing, justified right margin and a line length of 65 characters or 6.5". Save and print one copy.

SIERRA THEATRE BOOKINGS *centre and underscore*

During the past 6 months, there has been a considerable decrease in the income from theatre bookings. There may be a number of reasons for this decrease, but whatever the reason, we must try to reverse the trend.

One suggestion has been to reduce the prices for seats in certain parts of the house. To reduce the prices for Balcony seats would have the following effect on income.

Leave 1½"

The theory behind reducing the prices is quite simple. It is better to sell 500 seats at a lower price than 200 seats at a higher price.

I would recommend that we try this for an experimental period of say 1 month in February - normally the time when bookings are not very high. A comparison can then be made with last year's figures.

Task 2b

Recall the word processed document and in the space left, insert the extract from the spreadsheet from page 30, Task 17. Use either the cut and paste method, your integrated program, or desktop publishing.

Task 3a

Type a copy of the following document. Use single line spacing and a justified right margin. Save and print.

SIERRA PROPERTY COMPANY underscore & embolden

When looking for a property to buy, a number of factors need to be borne in mind. The first problem - is the property to be a house, bungalow or flat?

For some people, a flat is an ideal property, but there are not many available for sale in this area. The following is a list of the people who are looking for flats that we have on our books at the moment.

Leave 1½"

If you have decided against a flat, and have set your heart on a house or bungalow, it is important to consider whether or not you want a garden. A garden can mean a great deal of hard, but rewarding, work. A list of the current properties on our books with large gardens is given below:

Leave 1½"

Whatever your needs, you are sure to find a property to suit you at:

SIERRA PROPERTY COMPANY embolden

27 Chapman Place

RUNCORN WA7 2PQ

Telephone: 0928 456345

use double line spacing

Task 3b

Using either cut and paste or your integrated program, position the extracts from the database assignment, page 13, Tasks 6 and 7.

Task 4a

Type the following document in double line spacing with a justified right margin and a typing line of 65 characters (or 6.5"). Number each page. Save and print.

THE HOUSING MARKET centre

The housing market has not been as active this year as it has been in past years. We have a larger number of people on our boooks trying to sell their houses than there are people wishing to buy them.

We have a wide range of properties as shown in the following graph:

Start new page

Are you a first time buyer? If so, then come along and talk to us. We have on our books some small and reasonably priced properties.

Leave 2"

The above information shows the sort of property we can offer to those on a restricted budget. For example,

- low price
- small gardens
- 2 bedrooms

Task 4b

Using either cut and paste or your integrated program, first position the extract from the Graphics section, page 84 Task 5 at the end of page 1, or use a separate printout to create Appendix A. Secondly, position the extract from the Database Unit, page 14 Task 10, in the space provided on page 2 of your document.

Remember to repaginate the document as necessary.

Task 5a

Type a copy of the following document in double line spacing with a justified right margin. Number the pages. Save and print.

SIERRA CAR HIRE centre and embolden

The Company have decided to purchase 2 makes of car - the Pyramid and the Excelsior. These 2 makes have proved to be the most reliable over the past 3 years and to be the most popular with the hirers. This has been mainly because of the variety of models and the facilities offered. There are 10 models in the Pyramid range, ranging from the nippy 1.1 to the powerful 3.0. The cars are allocated to groups according to size and the following graph shows the number of models hired in the different groups available.

Start new page

Pick up/Drop off Points

As from the 1st January, we are offering a new service to our hirers. From that date the hirer of any car could decide where the car is picked up and dropped off when the period of hire is complete - they do not need to return the car to a set place.

Leave 1"

A number of hirers use our facilities for anywhere pick up as indicated above. A common pick up point is the airport or hotel and drop off at the same point.

Task 5b

Recall the word processed document. Either insert the graph from the Sierra Car Hire Assignment (page 80 Task 6) at the end of the text on page 1 or use a separate printout to create Appendix A. Remember to make any amendment to the text. Insert the extract from the database assignment (page 6 Task 9) in the space provided. Repaginate the document if necessary.

Task 6a

Type a copy of the following document in single line spacing, with a justified right margin. Save and print one copy.

BALANCING THE BUDGET centre, embolden, underline

Most people have to pay regular amounts out of their salary for such services as Gas, Electricity, Telephone, etc. It is vital that these bills are paid regularly and on time, otherwise the services are withdrawn. The results of withdrawal can be as catastrophic as losing one's home if the mortgage or rent has not been paid. There have been an increasing number of families who have been evicted because of non-payment.

It is therefore sensible to pay the mortgage as a priority and then to budget the remainder of the income. A simple budget can be written out - an example is shown below:

Leave 2½"

When the amount needed has been decided upon, it is then relatively easy to calculate the cash left over for other purchases.

If you are on a fixed income, it is often difficult to account for an increase in any of the bills.

Leave 2½"

The above shows the effect on the expenditure when a 10% overall increase has to be found from a fixed income.

Task 6b

Recall the word processed document, and using either cut and paste or your integrated program, insert the spreadsheet from page 19 Task 2 into the first space, and that from page 20 Task 6 into the second space.

Check carefully the space left - you may have to amend it to include the spreadsheets.

Task 7a

Type the following document, using double line spacing and a justified right margin. Set a line length of 65 spaces or 6.5". Number each page. Save and print one copy.

SIERRA THEATRE BOOKINGS emboldon

Methods of Payment

Over the past few years, the number of people making their bookings by telephone has increased considerably. This has followed the general increase in making payments of all kinds by credit card. Larger numbers of people are finding it easier and, for some purchases, possibly safer, to pay by credit card. If the amount owing is paid on receipt of the account, no interest charges are incurred, and therefore the price is not increased in any way.

The following Pie Chart shows the breakdown of the types of payments for all bookings:

New page

There are a number of areas of the United Kingdom which are covered by our booking agency. They vary considerably in the amount of bookings they make. A search was made of our database to find the number of bookings which were made by credit card by people living in Liverpool. The details are given below:

Leave 1½"

The extract given above shows that 3 bookings were made by credit card out of a total of 8 bookings for that period. Can we assume that these bookings would not have been made if the credit card facility had not been available?

Current Programme

The booking agency endeavours to offer seats for all types of play anywhere in the country.

Task 7a (cont)

We have discovered recently that there has been an upsurge in interest in the plays by Shakespeare, and this has been reflected in the number of his plays on offer throughout the country. The following is a list of the plays which are currently running, and for which we are now taking bookings:

Macbeth

The Tempest

Julius Caesar

Othello

<u>Macbeth</u> and <u>Othello</u> are sold out for the next two weeks, and there are limited seats available for <u>Julius Caesar</u> and <u>The Tempest</u>. We have never known a time when it has been advisable to book early for Shakespeare plays in the provinces.

Long may this trend continue! centre, embolden and underscore

Task 7 b

Recall the word processed document. Either insert the graph from the Sierra Bookings Assignment (page 82 Task 4) at the end of the text on Page 1 or use a separate printout to create Appendix A. Remember to make any necessary amendments to the text.

Insert the extract from the Sierra Bookings Database Assignment (page 10, Task 8) in the space provided.

Repaginate the document if necessary.

SOURCE DOCUMENTS

These sets of source documents contain the data necessary to complete many of the tasks set throughout this book. The student is directed to the required documents at the beginning of each set of tasks.

Source Documents A - Sierra Car Hire Company: Driver and Hire Details (pages 98 - 102).

Source Documents B - Sierra Theatre Bookings (pages 103 - 107).

Source Documents C - Sierra Property Company: Client and Property Details (pages 108 - 17).

SIERRA CAR HIRE - DRIVER AND HIRE DETAILS

Surname: MILLMAN
First Name: ANNE Other Initials: J
Group of Car: C Model of Car: EXCELSIOR 2.0
No of days: 8 Insurance premium paid: ~~YES~~/NO
Pick up from: Airport ✓ Harbour Hotel
Drop off at: Airport ✓ Harbour Hotel
Full cost: £228 Deposit: £45 Balance: £183

Signature: Date: 12/1

SIERRA CAR HIRE - DRIVER AND HIRE DETAILS

Surname: CHANNON
First Name: MARGARET Other Initials: A
Group of Car: C Model of Car: PYRAMID 2.3
No of days: 7 Insurance premium paid: YES/~~NO~~
Pick up from: Airport Harbour Hotel ✓
Drop off at: Airport Harbour Hotel ✓
Full cost: £ 225 Deposit: £ 45 Balance: £180

Signature: Date: 12/1

SIERRA CAR HIRE - DRIVER AND HIRE DETAILS

Surname: CULHANE
First Name: BARBARA Other Initials: M
Group of Car: A Model of Car: PYRAMID 1.3
No of days: 15 Insurance premium paid: ~~YES~~/NO
Pick up from: Airport Harbour ✓ Hotel
Drop off at: Airport Harbour ✓ Hotel
Full cost: £ 290 Deposit: £ 60 Balance: £230

Signature: Date: 14/1

SIERRA CAR HIRE - DRIVER AND HIRE DETAILS

Surname: RIX
First Name: ALEX Other Initials:
Group of Car: E Model of Car: EXCELSIOR 3.0
No of days: 5 Insurance premium paid: ~~YES~~/NO
Pick up from: Airport Harbour Hotel ✓
Drop off at: Airport ✓ Harbour Hotel
Full cost: £ 175 Deposit: £ 35 Balance: £140

Signature: Date: 13/1

SIERRA CAR HIRE - DRIVER AND HIRE DETAILS

Surname: HANNON
First Name: ROGER Other Initials:
Group of Car: D Model of Car: PYRAMID 2.9
No of days: 7 Insurance premium paid: YES/~~NO~~
Pick up from: Airport ✓ Harbour Hotel
Drop off at: Airport Harbour ✓ Hotel
Full cost: £245 Deposit: £50 Balance: £195

Signature: Date: 16/1

SIERRA CAR HIRE - DRIVER AND HIRE DETAILS

Surname: SHORTE
First Name: MALCOLM Other Initials:
Group of Car: C Model of Car: EXCELSIOR 1.8
No of days: 12 Insurance premium paid: ~~YES~~/NO
Pick up from: Airport Harbour Hotel ✓
Drop off at: Airport Harbour Hotel ✓
Full cost: £300 Deposit: £60 Balance: £240

Signature: Date: 15/1

SIERRA CAR HIRE - DRIVER AND HIRE DETAILS

Surname: AKEHURST
First Name: ROBERTA Other Initials: L
Group of Car: B Model of Car: EXCELSIOR 1.4
No of days: 2 Insurance premium paid: YES/~~NO~~
Pick up from: Airport Harbour Hotel ✓
Drop off at: Airport Harbour Hotel ✓
Full cost: £46.50 Deposit: £10 Balance: £36.50

Signature: Date: 13/1

SIERRA CAR HIRE - DRIVER AND HIRE DETAILS

Surname: COLE
First Name: CORRINNE Other Initials:
Group of Car: C Model of Car: PYRAMID 1.8
No of days: 9 Insurance premium paid: ~~YES~~/NO
Pick up from: Airport Harbour Hotel ✓
Drop off at: Airport ✓ Harbour Hotel
Full cost: £225 Deposit: £45 Balance: £180

Signature: Date: 16/1

SIERRA CAR HIRE - DRIVER AND HIRE DETAILS

Surname: BRITTAIN
First Name: GENEVIEVE Other Initials: K
Group of Car: C Model of Car: PYRAMID 1.8
No of days: 7 Insurance premium paid: YES/~~NO~~
Pick up from: Airport ✓ Harbour Hotel
Drop off at: Airport Harbour Hotel ✓
Full cost: £ 175 Deposit: £ 35 Balance: £ 140

Signature: Date: 12/1

SIERRA CAR HIRE - DRIVER AND HIRE DETAILS

Surname: ELSWORTH
First Name: Pamela Other Initials: T
Group of Car: C Model of Car: PYRAMID 2.3
No of days: 3 Insurance premium paid: ~~YES~~/NO
Pick up from: Airport Harbour ✓ Hotel
Drop off at: Airport Harbour ✓ Hotel
Full cost: £ 70 Deposit: £ 15 Balance: £ 55

Signature: Date: 14/1

SIERRA CAR HIRE - DRIVER AND HIRE DETAILS

Surname: OWEN
First Name: ELAINE Other Initials: K
Group of Car: C Model of Car: EXCELSIOR 1.8
No of days: 9 Insurance premium paid: ~~YES~~/NO
Pick up from: Airport ✓ Harbour Hotel
Drop off at: Airport ✓ Harbour Hotel
Full cost: £ 225 Deposit: £ 45 Balance: £ 180

Signature: Date: 13/1

SIERRA CAR HIRE - DRIVER AND HIRE DETAILS

Surname: SLACK
First Name: TERESA Other Initials: G
Group of Car: B Model of Car: PYRAMID 1.5
No of days: 7 Insurance premium paid: YES/~~NO~~
Pick up from: Airport Harbour Hotel ✓
Drop off at: Airport Harbour Hotel ✓
Full cost: £ 150 Deposit: £ 30 Balance: £ 120

Signature: Date: 14/1

SIERRA CAR HIRE - DRIVER AND HIRE DETAILS

Surname: SMITHSON
First Name: PHILIP Other Initials: A
Group of Car: A Model of Car: EXCELSIOR 1.1
No of days: 5 Insurance premium paid: ~~YES~~/NO
Pick up from: Airport ✓ Harbour Hotel
Drop off at: Airport ✓ Harbour Hotel
Full cost: £ 90 Deposit: £ 20 Balance: £70

Signature: Date: 14/1

SIERRA CAR HIRE - DRIVER AND HIRE DETAILS

Surname: SELKIRK
First Name: ANDREW Other Initials:
Group of Car: D Model of Car: PYRAMID 2.9
No of days: 12 Insurance premium paid: YES/~~NO~~
Pick up from: Airport Harbour ✓ Hotel
Drop off at: Airport Harbour ✓ Hotel
Full cost: £ 420 Deposit: £ 85 Balance: £335

Signature: Date: 17/1

SIERRA CAR HIRE - DRIVER AND HIRE DETAILS

Surname: QUINLAN
First Name: TERENCE Other Initials: J
Group of Car: C Model of Car: PYRAMID 2.3
No of days: 8 Insurance premium paid: ~~YES~~/NO
Pick up from: Airport Harbour Hotel ✓
Drop off at: Airport Harbour Hotel ✓
Full cost: £257 Deposit: £ 50 Balance: £207

Signature: Date: 21/1

SIERRA CAR HIRE - DRIVER AND HIRE DETAILS

Surname: HOLLINSHEAD
First Name: CHRISTOPHER Other Initials: P
Group of Car: C Model of Car: PYRAMID 2.0
No of days: 3 Insurance premium paid: YES/~~NO~~
Pick up from: Airport Harbour Hotel ✓
Drop off at: Airport ✓ Harbour Hotel
Full cost: £95 Deposit: £ 20 Balance: £75

Signature: Date: 16/1

SIERRA CAR HIRE - DRIVER AND HIRE DETAILS

Surname: MASSIN
First Name: MOUBARAK Other Initials:
Group of Car: B Model of Car: EXCELSIOR 1.6
No of days: 7 Insurance premium paid: YES/~~NO~~
Pick up from: Airport Harbour ✓ Hotel
Drop off at: Airport Harbour ✓ Hotel
Full cost: £ 160 Deposit: £ 35 Balance: £ 125

Signature: Date: 19/1

SIERRA CAR HIRE - DRIVER AND HIRE DETAILS

Surname: SPANN
First Name: ANDREAS Other Initials: A
Group of Car: C Model of Car: PYRAMID 2.0
No of days: 12 Insurance premium paid: ~~YES~~/NO
Pick up from: Airport ✓ Harbour Hotel
Drop off at: Airport Harbour Hotel ✓
Full cost: £ 340 Deposit: £ 70 Balance: £270

Signature: Date: 16/1

SIERRA CAR HIRE - DRIVER AND HIRE DETAILS

Surname: THOMPSON
First Name: PHILIP Other Initials: N
Group of Car: C Model of Car: PYRAMID 2.3
No of days: 9 Insurance premium paid: YES/~~NO~~
Pick up from: Airport Harbour ✓ Hotel
Drop off at: Airport Harbour ✓ Hotel
Full cost: £ 225 Deposit: £ 45 Balance: £180

Signature: Date: 17/1

SIERRA CAR HIRE - DRIVER AND HIRE DETAILS

Surname: PETERSON
First Name: KENNETH Other Initials: L
Group of Car: B Model of Car: EXCELSIOR 1.6
No of days: 7 Insurance premium paid: YES/~~NO~~
Pick up from: Airport ✓ Harbour Hotel
Drop off at: Airport Harbour Hotel ✓
Full cost: £ 160 Deposit: £ 35 Balance: £125

Signature: Date: 23/1

SIERRA THEATRE BOOKINGS

Name: SHAKIL, AMAR
Address: 80 GRANGE GROVE
Town: LIVERPOOL Postcode: LN7 1KP
Name of Show: THE TEMPEST
Date of Show: 20/1 Seats: CIRCLE
No of Tickets: Adults 4 Children 0
Payment: ~~Cash / Credit Card~~ / Cheque
Amount: £48
Credit Card No:
Expiry Date:

SIERRA THEATRE BOOKINGS

Name: SHAWANI, ABDUL
Address: 149 GIRTRELL ROAD
Town: WARRINGTON Postcode: WN7 1AG
Name of Show: THE TEMPEST
Date of Show: 15/1 Seats: STALLS
No of Tickets: Adults 2 Children 4
Payment: ~~Cash~~ / Credit Card / ~~Cheque~~
Amount: £62
Credit Card No: 123 387 471 371
Expiry Date: 3/

SIERRA THEATRE BOOKINGS

Name: DOYLE, ANGUS
Address: 10 RONSON STREET
Town: MANCHESTER Postcode: MN10 1EP
Name of Show: OTHELLO
Date of Show: 23/1 Seats: BALCONY
No of Tickets: Adults 4 Children 20
Payment: ~~Cash~~ / Credit Card / ~~Cheque~~
Amount: £160
Credit Card No: 123 522 430 856
Expiry Date: 12/

SIERRA THEATRE BOOKINGS

Name: ARROWE, ISAAC
Address: 33 WILLISTON DRIVE
Town: LIVERPOOL Postcode: LN6 1KC
Name of Show: THE TEMPEST
Date of Show: 18/1 Seats: CIRCLE
No of Tickets: Adults 3 Children 0
Payment: ~~Cash / Credit Card~~ / Cheque
Amount: £36
Credit Card No:
Expiry Date:

SIERRA THEATRE BOOKINGS
Name: BRADBOURNE, EDWARD
Address: 58 Singleton Avenue
Town: Warrington Postcode: WN4 9DE
Name of Show: Macbeth
Date of Show: 26/1 Seats: Stalls
No of Tickets: Adults 2 Children 4
Payment: ~~Cash~~ / Credit Card / ~~Cheque~~
Amount: £88
Credit Card No: 5224 3689 9683 4212
Expiry Date: 6/

SIERRA THEATRE BOOKINGS
Name: ROACH, Margaret
Address: 25 Franklyn Close
Town: Liverpool Postcode: LV6 2EF
Name of Show: THE TEMPEST
Date of Show: 16/1 Seats: CIRCLE
No of Tickets: Adults 2 Children 3
Payment: ~~Cash / Credit Card~~ / Cheque
Amount: £45
Credit Card No:
Expiry Date:

SIERRA THEATRE BOOKINGS
Name: MASON, TERESA
Address: 9 BULWER STREET
Town: ELLESMERE PORT Postcode: EL6 8ZJ
Name of Show: The Tempest
Date of Show: 24/1 Seats: Balcony
No of Tickets: Adults 6 Children 15
Payment: ~~Cash / Credit Card~~ / Cheque
Amount: £150
Credit Card No:
Expiry Date:

SIERRA THEATRE BOOKINGS
Name: CROPPER, Ian
Address: 250 SHIP STREET
Town: MANCHESTER Postcode: MN1 8FG
Name of Show: Julius Caesar
Date of Show: 19/1 Seats: STALLS
No of Tickets: Adults 3 Children 10
Payment: ~~Cash~~ / Credit Card / ~~Cheque~~
Amount: £180
Credit Card No: 123 781 135 888
Expiry Date: 6/

SIERRA THEATRE BOOKINGS
Name: UNSWORTH, NORMA
Address: 6 MARLBOROUGH DRIVE
Town: LIVERPOOL Postcode: LV10 5KG
Name of Show: OTHELLO
Date of Show: 28/1 Seats: STALLS
No of Tickets: Adults 2 Children 0
Payment: Cash / ~~Credit Card / Cheque~~
Amount: £35
Credit Card No:
Expiry Date:

SIERRA THEATRE BOOKINGS
Name: BOYD, HENRIETTA
Address: 126 BOYER AVENUE
Town: ELLESMERE PORT Postcode: EP5 8LJ
Name of Show: THE TEMPEST
Date of Show: 17/1 Seats: BALCONY
No of Tickets: Adults 2 Children 4
Payment: ~~Cash / Credit Card~~ / Cheque
Amount: £44
Credit Card No:
Expiry Date:

SIERRA THEATRE BOOKINGS
Name: ROOKE, Brian
Address: 55 Millhouse Lane
Town: Liverpool Postcode: LV11 4KJ
Name of Show: Julius Caesar
Date of Show: 25/1 Seats: Balcony
No of Tickets: Adults 4 Children 10
Payment: ~~Cash~~ / Credit Card / ~~Cheque~~
Amount: £118
Credit Card No: 123 917 444 888
Expiry Date: 7/

SIERRA THEATRE BOOKINGS
Name: JUDD, Leonard
Address: 22 Green Lane
Town: Manchester Postcode: MN1 7LT
Name of Show: The Tempest
Date of Show: 22/1 Seats: Circle
No of Tickets: Adults 2 Children 3
Payment: ~~Cash~~ / Credit Card / ~~Cheque~~
Amount: £45
Credit Card No: 5224 8118 4647 9314
Expiry Date: 5/

SIERRA THEATRE BOOKINGS
Name: ELLISON, W M
Address: 64 TERRET CLOSE
Town: LIVERPOOL Postcode: LN9 9FW
Name of Show: THE TEMPEST
Date of Show: 30/1 Seats: BALCONY
No of Tickets: Adults 6 Children 24
Payment: ~~Cash~~ / Credit Card / ~~Cheque~~
Amount: £204
Credit Card No: 123 327 285 402
Expiry Date: 12/

SIERRA THEATRE BOOKINGS
Name: LEE, ARTHUR
Address: 10 INCE ROAD
Town: MANCHESTER Postcode: MT5 7QM
Name of Show: JULIUS CAESAR
Date of Show: 15/1 Seats: STALLS
No of Tickets: Adults 2 Children 2
Payment: Cash / ~~Credit Card / Cheque~~
Amount: £64
Credit Card No:
Expiry Date:

SIERRA THEATRE BOOKINGS
Name: SAKER, PETER
Address: 74 MARITIME CLOSE
Town: WARRINGTON Postcode: WN2 8BC
Name of Show: OTHELLO
Date of Show: 21/1 Seats: CIRCLE
No of Tickets: Adults 3 Children 6
Payment: ~~Cash~~ / Credit Card / ~~Cheque~~
Amount: £84
Credit Card No: 123 981 361 878
Expiry Date: 9/

SIERRA THEATRE BOOKINGS
Name: DANIELS, Michael
Address: 99 NEVILLE AVENUE
Town: ELLESMERE PORT Postcode: EP10 7EG
Name of Show: JULIUS CAESAR
Date of Show: 21/1 Seats: STALLS
No of Tickets: Adults 4 Children 0
Payment: ~~Cash / Credit Card~~ / Cheque
Amount: £80
Credit Card No:
Expiry Date:

SIERRA THEATRE BOOKINGS
Name: BYRNE, PETER
Address: 18 PARK ROAD
Town: LIVERPOOL Postcode: LV6 2QL
Name of Show: THE TEMPEST
Date of Show: 16/1 Seats: STALLS
No of Tickets: Adults 2 Children 2
Payment: Cash / ~~Credit Card / Cheque~~
Amount: £46
Credit Card No:
Expiry Date:

SIERRA THEATRE BOOKINGS
Name: HARDY, ALAN
Address: 142 CHATSWORTH PLACE
Town: MANCHESTER Postcode: MN2 3DL
Name of Show: THE TEMPEST
Date of Show: 21/1 Seats: CIRCLE
No of Tickets: Adults 2 Children 6
Payment: Cash / ~~Credit Card / Cheque~~
Amount: £66
Credit Card No:
Expiry Date:

SIERRA THEATRE BOOKINGS
Name: NASH, CHRISTINA
Address: 35 CAVELL CLOSE
Town: WARRINGTON Postcode: WN4 5T2
Name of Show: OTHELLO
Date of Show: 17/1 Seats: BALCONY
No of Tickets: Adults 3 Children 12
Payment: ~~Cash~~ / Credit Card / ~~Cheque~~
Amount: £102
Credit Card No: 617 217 338 456
Expiry Date: 5/

SIERRA THEATRE BOOKINGS
Name: CUNNINGHAM, JOHN
Address: 10 LINGFIELD ROAD
Town: LIVERPOOL Postcode: LT8 4PZ
Name of Show: MACBETH
Date of Show: 30/1 Seats: STALLS
No of Tickets: Adults 3 Children 0
Payment: ~~Cash~~ / Credit Card / ~~Cheque~~
Amount: £60
Credit Card No: 5224 7215 8643 1789
Expiry Date: 4/

SIERRA PROPERTY CO

If you wish to buy a new property, the completion of the following details will assist us in helping you to find your dream home.

Name: BOWYER, ANDREW

Address: 32 QUEENS AVE

Town: EXFIELD

Postcode: EXT 4LM Tel No: 52422

Price: Minimum £ 35,000 Maximum £ 50,000

TYPE OF PROPERTY TO BE PURCHASED

House: Semi ✓ Detached Terraced

Flat:

Bungalow: Semi Detached Terraced

Minimum No of: Bedrooms 2 Reception Rooms 1

Garden: Large Small ✓ None

CURRENT PROPERTY

Do you have a property to sell: Yes No ✓

Are you a First Time Buyer: Yes No

House: Semi Detached Terraced

Flat:

Bungalow: Semi Detached Dormer

No of: Bedrooms Reception Rooms

Garden: Large Small None

Do you require details of mortgage facilities: ~~YES~~ / NO

Signed:

Date: 18/1

SIERRA PROPERTY CO

If you wish to buy a new property, the completion of the following details will assist us in helping you to find your dream home.

Name: MAKIN, PHILIP

Address: 39 BELLMORE AVE

Town: HALTON

Postcode: HN6 3GE Tel No: 261333

Price: Minimum £ 50,000 Maximum £ 60,000

TYPE OF PROPERTY TO BE PURCHASED

House: Semi ✓ Detached Terraced

Flat:

Bungalow: Semi Detached Terraced

Minimum No of: Bedrooms 2 Reception Rooms 2

Garden: Large Small ✓ None

CURRENT PROPERTY

Do you have a property to sell: Yes ✓ No

Are you a First Time Buyer: Yes No

House: Semi ✓ Detached Terraced

Flat:

Bungalow: Semi Detached Dormer

No of: Bedrooms 2 Reception Rooms 1

Garden: Large Small None ✓

Do you require details of mortgage facilities: YES / ~~NO~~

Signed:

Date: 19/1

SIERRA PROPERTY CO

If you wish to buy a new property, the completion of the following details will assist us in helping you to find your dream home.

Name: SARTOVIS, DENNIS

Address: 130 GABLES ROAD

Town: EXFIELD

Postcode: EX7 7AG Tel No: 56192

Price: Minimum £ 65,000 Maximum £100,000

TYPE OF PROPERTY TO BE PURCHASED

House: Semi Detached ✓ Terraced

Flat:

Bungalow: Semi Detached Terraced

Minimum No of: Bedrooms 3 Reception Rooms 2

Garden: Large ✓ Small None

CURRENT PROPERTY

Do you have a property to sell: Yes ✓ No

Are you a First Time Buyer: Yes No

House: Semi Detached Terraced ✓

Flat:

Bungalow: Semi Detached Dormer

No of: Bedrooms 3 Reception Rooms 1

Garden: Large Small None ✓

Do you require details of mortgage facilities: ~~YES~~ / NO

Signed:

Date: 17/1

SIERRA PROPERTY CO

If you wish to buy a new property, the completion of the following details will assist us in helping you to find your dream home.

Name: SAUNDERS, CHARLES

Address: 380 GARTH AVENUE

Town: EXFIELD

Postcode: EX7 1LM Tel No: 56727

Price: Minimum £ 60,000 Maximum £ 80,000

TYPE OF PROPERTY TO BE PURCHASED

House: Semi Detached Terraced

Flat:

Bungalow: Semi Detached ✓ Terraced

Minimum No of: Bedrooms 2 Reception Rooms 2

Garden: Large ✓ Small None

CURRENT PROPERTY

Do you have a property to sell: Yes ✓ No

Are you a First Time Buyer: Yes No

House: Semi Detached ✓ Terraced

Flat:

Bungalow: Semi Detached Dormer

No of: Bedrooms 2 Reception Rooms 1

Garden: Large Small ✓ None

Do you require details of mortgage facilities: YES / ~~NO~~

Signed:

Date: 17/1

SIERRA PROPERTY CO

If you wish to buy a new property, the completion of the following details will assist us in helping you to find your dream home.

Name: HEGARTY, ALEC THOMAS
Address: 10 UPPINGHAM DRIVE
Town: EXFIELD
Postcode: EX7 7BK   Tel No: 52313
Price: Minimum £ 45,000   Maximum £ 65,000

TYPE OF PROPERTY TO BE PURCHASED
House: Semi   Detached ✓   Terraced
Flat:
Bungalow: Semi   Detached   Terraced
Minimum No of: Bedrooms 3   Reception Rooms 2
Garden: Large ✓   Small   None

CURRENT PROPERTY
Do you have a property to sell: Yes ✓   No
Are you a First Time Buyer: Yes   No
House: Semi   Detached   Terraced ✓
Flat:
Bungalow: Semi   Detached   Dormer
No of: Bedrooms 2   Reception Rooms 1
Garden: Large   Small   None ✓
Do you require details of mortgage facilities: YES / ~~NO~~
Signed:
Date: 16/1

SIERRA PROPERTY CO

If you wish to buy a new property, the completion of the following details will assist us in helping you to find your dream home.

Name: POSTLETHWAITE, VIRGINIA
Address: 3 WALLACE TERRACE
Town: WESTON
Postcode: WN12 4LD   Tel No: 662517
Price: Minimum £ 35,000   Maximum £ 45,000

TYPE OF PROPERTY TO BE PURCHASED
House: Semi   Detached   Terraced
Flat: ✓
Bungalow: Semi   Detached   Terraced
Minimum No of: Bedrooms 2   Reception Rooms 1
Garden: Large   Small   None ✓

CURRENT PROPERTY
Do you have a property to sell: Yes   No
Are you a First Time Buyer: Yes ✓   No
House: Semi   Detached   Terraced
Flat:
Bungalow: Semi   Detached   Dormer
No of: Bedrooms   Reception Rooms
Garden: Large   Small   None
Do you require details of mortgage facilities: YES / ~~NO~~
Signed:
Date: 16/1

SIERRA PROPERTY CO

If you wish to buy a new property, the completion of the following details will assist us in helping you to find your dream home.

Name: INGERSEN, HENRY

Address: 91 OXTON RD

Town: HALTON

Postcode: HN6 4LD Tel No: 225161

Price: Minimum £ 25,000 Maximum £40,000

TYPE OF PROPERTY TO BE PURCHASED

House: Semi Detached Terraced ✓

Flat:

Bungalow: Semi Detached Terraced

Minimum No of: Bedrooms 2 Reception Rooms 1

Garden: Large Small None ✓

CURRENT PROPERTY

Do you have a property to sell: Yes No

Are you a First Time Buyer: Yes ✓ No

House: Semi Detached Terraced

Flat:

Bungalow: Semi Detached Dormer

No of: Bedrooms Reception Rooms

Garden: Large Small None

Do you require details of mortgage facilities: YES / ~~NO~~

Signed:

Date: 20/1

SIERRA PROPERTY CO

If you wish to buy a new property, the completion of the following details will assist us in helping you to find your dream home.

Name: HAGGETT, CHRISTINE

Address: 19 BURNTREE CLOSE

Town: EXFIELD

Postcode: EX7 1PO Tel No: 57811

Price: Minimum £ 50,000 Maximum £ 70,000

TYPE OF PROPERTY TO BE PURCHASED

House: Semi Detached ✓ Terraced

Flat:

Bungalow: Semi Detached Terraced

Minimum No of: Bedrooms 3 Reception Rooms 2

Garden: Large ✓ Small None

CURRENT PROPERTY

Do you have a property to sell: Yes ✓ No

Are you a First Time Buyer: Yes No

House: Semi ✓ Detached Terraced

Flat:

Bungalow: Semi Detached Dormer

No of: Bedrooms 2 Reception Rooms 2

Garden: Large Small ✓ None

Do you require details of mortgage facilities: ~~YES~~ / NO

Signed:

Date: 17/1

SIERRA PROPERTY CO

If you wish to buy a new property, the completion of the following details will assist us in helping you to find your dream home.

Name: KAVANAGH, STANLEY

Address: 71 BOGNOR CLOSE

Town: EXFIELD

Postcode: EX7 1KD Tel No: 56161

Price: Minimum £ 90,000 Maximum £120,000

TYPE OF PROPERTY TO BE PURCHASED

House: Semi Detached ✓ Terraced

Flat:

Bungalow: Semi Detached Terraced

Minimum No of: Bedrooms 5 Reception Rooms 3

Garden: Large ✓ Small None

CURRENT PROPERTY

Do you have a property to sell: Yes ✓ No

Are you a First Time Buyer: Yes No

House: Semi Detached Terraced

Flat:

Bungalow: Semi Detached ✓ Dormer

No of: Bedrooms 3 Reception Rooms 2

Garden: Large Small ✓ None

Do you require details of mortgage facilities: ~~YES~~ / NO

Signed:

Date: 18/1

SIERRA PROPERTY CO

If you wish to buy a new property, the completion of the following details will assist us in helping you to find your dream home.

Name: ILLSLEY, PETER

Address: 44 MARSH HOUSE LANE

Town: HALTON

Postcode: HN6 1TD Tel No: 273361

Price: Minimum £ 125,000 Maximum £ 150,000

TYPE OF PROPERTY TO BE PURCHASED

House: Semi Detached Terraced

Flat:

Bungalow: Semi Detached ✓ Terraced

Minimum No of: Bedrooms 4 Reception Rooms 3

Garden: Large ✓ Small None

CURRENT PROPERTY

Do you have a property to sell: Yes ✓ No

Are you a First Time Buyer: Yes No

House: Semi Detached ✓ Terraced

Flat:

Bungalow: Semi Detached Dormer

No of: Bedrooms 3 Reception Rooms 2

Garden: Large Small ✓ None

Do you require details of mortgage facilities: YES / ~~NO~~

Signed:

Date: 19/1

SIERRA PROPERTY CO

If you wish to buy a new property, the completion of the following details will assist us in helping you to find your dream home.

Name: LLEWELLYN, GWYNNETH

Address: 29 BROOKSIDE ROAD

Town: EXFIELD

Postcode: EX7 8BP Tel No: 51985

Price: Minimum £ 60,000 Maximum £ 70,000

TYPE OF PROPERTY TO BE PURCHASED

House: Semi Detached Terraced

Flat:

Bungalow: Semi Detached ✓ Terraced

Minimum No of: Bedrooms 2 Reception Rooms 1

Garden: Large ✓ Small None

CURRENT PROPERTY

Do you have a property to sell: Yes No ✓

Are you a First Time Buyer: Yes No

House: Semi Detached Terraced

Flat:

Bungalow: Semi Detached Dormer

No of: Bedrooms Reception Rooms

Garden: Large Small None

Do you require details of mortgage facilities: ~~YES~~ / NO

Signed:

Date: 18/1

SIERRA PROPERTY CO

If you wish to buy a new property, the completion of the following details will assist us in helping you to find your dream home.

Name: LEWIS, BRIAN

Address: 96 EMMERDALE WAY

Town: PRINCETON

Postcode: PR4 2PQ Tel No: 85612

Price: Minimum £ 70,000 Maximum £ 100,000

TYPE OF PROPERTY TO BE PURCHASED

House: Semi Detached Terraced

Flat:

Bungalow: Semi Detached ✓ Terraced

Minimum No of: Bedrooms 4 Reception Rooms 3

Garden: Large ✓ Small None

CURRENT PROPERTY

Do you have a property to sell: Yes No ✓

Are you a First Time Buyer: Yes No

House: Semi Detached Terraced

Flat:

Bungalow: Semi Detached Dormer

No of: Bedrooms Reception Rooms

Garden: Large Small None

Do you require details of mortgage facilities: YES / ~~NO~~

Signed:

Date: 17/1

SIERRA PROPERTY CO

If you wish to buy a new property, the completion of the following details will assist us in helping you to find your dream home.

Name: HOLYCROFT, JOHN H

Address: 47 WORTHING ST

Town: EXFIELD

Postcode: EX7 7DH Tel No: 52765

Price: Minimum £ 45,000 Maximum £ 60,000

TYPE OF PROPERTY TO BE PURCHASED

House: Semi Detached ✓ Terraced

Flat:

Bungalow: Semi Detached Terraced

Minimum No of: Bedrooms 3 Reception Rooms 2

Garden: Large Small ✓ None

CURRENT PROPERTY

Do you have a property to sell: Yes ✓ No

Are you a First Time Buyer: Yes No

House: Semi ✓ Detached Terraced

Flat:

Bungalow: Semi Detached Dormer

No of: Bedrooms 2 Reception Rooms 1

Garden: Large Small None ✓

Do you require details of mortgage facilities: YES / ~~NO~~

Signed:

Date: 18/1

SIERRA PROPERTY CO

If you wish to buy a new property, the completion of the following details will assist us in helping you to find your dream home.

Name: JUKES, KAREN GILLIAN

Address: 57 SEFTON STREET

Town: HALTON

Postcode: HN6 7DT Tel No: 238715

Price: Minimum £ 75,000 Maximum £ 85,000

TYPE OF PROPERTY TO BE PURCHASED

House: Semi Detached Terraced

Flat:

Bungalow: Semi Detached Terraced ✓

Minimum No of: Bedrooms 3 Reception Rooms 2

Garden: Large Small ✓ None

CURRENT PROPERTY

Do you have a property to sell: Yes No

Are you a First Time Buyer: Yes ✓ No

House: Semi Detached Terraced

Flat:

Bungalow: Semi Detached Dormer

No of: Bedrooms Reception Rooms

Garden: Large Small None

Do you require details of mortgage facilities: YES / ~~NO~~

Signed:

Date: 19/1

SIERRA PROPERTY CO

If you wish to buy a new property, the completion of the following details will assist us in helping you to find your dream home.

Name: CANNELL, TERENCE

Address: 18 ROSEBERRY GARDENS

Town: EXFIELD

Postcode: EX7 6TQ Tel No: 51795

Price: Minimum £ 50,000 Maximum £ 75,000

TYPE OF PROPERTY TO BE PURCHASED

House: Semi ✓ Detached Terraced

Flat:

Bungalow: Semi Detached Terraced

Minimum No of: Bedrooms 3 Reception Rooms 1

Garden: Large Small ✓ None

CURRENT PROPERTY

Do you have a property to sell: Yes ✓ No

Are you a First Time Buyer: Yes No

House: Semi ✓ Detached Terraced

Flat:

Bungalow: Semi Detached Dormer

No of: Bedrooms 2 Reception Rooms 1

Garden: Large Small None ✓

Do you require details of mortgage facilities: YES / ~~NO~~

Signed:

Date: 18/1

SIERRA PROPERTY CO

If you wish to buy a new property, the completion of the following details will assist us in helping you to find your dream home.

Name: HARRISON, JAMES

Address: 21 VOSE CLOSE

Town: EXFIELD

Postcode: EX7 8AB Tel No: 52261

Price: Minimum £ 50,000 Maximum £ 65,000

TYPE OF PROPERTY TO BE PURCHASED

House: Semi Detached ✓ Terraced

Flat:

Bungalow: Semi Detached Terraced

Minimum No of: Bedrooms 3 Reception Rooms 2

Garden: Large Small ✓ None

CURRENT PROPERTY

Do you have a property to sell: Yes No

Are you a First Time Buyer: Yes ✓ No

House: Semi Detached Terraced

Flat:

Bungalow: Semi Detached Dormer

No of: Bedrooms Reception Rooms

Garden: Large Small None

Do you require details of mortgage facilities: ~~YES~~ / NO

Signed:

Date: 19/1

SIERRA PROPERTY CO

If you wish to buy a new property, the completion of the following details will assist us in helping you to find your dream home.

Name: FORBES, BELINDA JANE

Address: 42 CRANLOCK CLOSE

Town: HALTON

Postcode: HN6 7EC Tel No: 219981

Price: Minimum £ 100,000 Maximum £ 125,000

TYPE OF PROPERTY TO BE PURCHASED

House: Semi Detached ✓ Terraced

Flat:

Bungalow: Semi Detached Terraced

Minimum No of: Bedrooms 5 Reception Rooms 3

Garden: Large ✓ Small None

CURRENT PROPERTY

Do you have a property to sell: Yes ✓ No

Are you a First Time Buyer: Yes No

House: Semi Detached ✓ Terraced

Flat:

Bungalow: Semi Detached Dormer

No of: Bedrooms 3 Reception Rooms 2

Garden: Large Small ✓ None

Do you require details of mortgage facilities: YES / ~~NO~~

Signed:

Date: 17/1

SIERRA PROPERTY CO

If you wish to buy a new property, the completion of the following details will assist us in helping you to find your dream home.

Name: ELLISON, JOHN W

Address: 39 HILLSIDE RD

Town: EXFIELD

Postcode: EX7 1TD Tel No: 54781

Price: Minimum £ 30,000 Maximum £ 45,000

TYPE OF PROPERTY TO BE PURCHASED

House: Semi Detached Terraced

Flat: ✓

Bungalow: Semi Detached Terraced

Minimum No of: Bedrooms 2 Reception Rooms 1

Garden: Large Small None ✓

CURRENT PROPERTY

Do you have a property to sell: Yes No

Are you a First Time Buyer: Yes ✓ No

House: Semi Detached Terraced

Flat:

Bungalow: Semi Detached Dormer

No of: Bedrooms Reception Rooms

Garden: Large Small None

Do you require details of mortgage facilities: ~~YES~~ / NO

Signed:

Date: 20/1

SIERRA PROPERTY CO

If you wish to buy a new property, the completion of the following details will assist us in helping you to find your dream home.

Name: OWEN, SIMON

Address: 15 BRADDON ROAD

Town: WESTON

Postcode: WN12 4TQ Tel No: 621789

Price: Minimum £ 50,000 Maximum £ 60,000

TYPE OF PROPERTY TO BE PURCHASED

House: Semi Detached Terraced ✓

Flat:

Bungalow: Semi Detached Terraced

Minimum No of: Bedrooms 2 Reception Rooms 1

Garden: Large Small None ✓

CURRENT PROPERTY

Do you have a property to sell: Yes ✓ No

Are you a First Time Buyer: Yes No

House: Semi Detached Terraced

Flat: ✓

Bungalow: Semi Detached Dormer

No of: Bedrooms 1 Reception Rooms 1

Garden: Large Small None 1

Do you require details of mortgage facilities: ~~YES~~ / NO

Signed:

Date: 16/1

SIERRA PROPERTY CO

If you wish to buy a new property, the completion of the following details will assist us in helping you to find your dream home.

Name: GLENNARD, ANNE-MARIE

Address: 25 ST JOHN'S ROAD

Town: HALTON

Postcode: HN6 4AE Tel No: 217832

Price: Minimum £ 125,000 Maximum £ 150,000

TYPE OF PROPERTY TO BE PURCHASED

House: Semi Detached ✓ Terraced

Flat:

Bungalow: Semi Detached Terraced

Minimum No of: Bedrooms 6 Reception Rooms 3

Garden: Large ✓ Small None

CURRENT PROPERTY

Do you have a property to sell: Yes ✓ No

Are you a First Time Buyer: Yes No

House: Semi ✓ Detached Terraced

Flat:

Bungalow: Semi Detached Dormer

No of: Bedrooms 4 Reception Rooms 2

Garden: Large ✓ Small None

Do you require details of mortgage facilities: ~~YES~~ / NO

Signed:

Date: 17/1

ASSIGNMENT 1

DATABASE

1 Using the information on the enrolment forms (pages 125 - 34), set up a database of the enrolments for the three months, 1st April to 30th June. Include the following fields in the database.

COURSE
CODE NO
VENUE
CONFIRMATION NO
DELEGATE'S NAME
TEL NO
COST
METHOD OF PAYMENT

2 Extract the relevant data from the enrolment forms and enter it into the database.

3 Save the data.

4 Print the data.

5 Sort the list into ascending order of confirmation number.

6 Save the list in the sorted version and print one copy.

7 Search the file for all those who enrolled for DTP courses in Liverpool and who paid by credit card.

8 Save the results of the search in step 7 and print CONFIRMATION NO, DELEGATE'S NAME, TEL NO and COST.

SPREADSHEET

1 Create a spreadsheet using the data on the enrolment forms (pages 125 - 34) and on the Data Sheet (page 124). The title of the spreadsheet should be BALFOUR SEMINARS - ANNUAL STATISTICS.

Use the following column headings:

COURSE
COST PER COURSE
1ST QTR
2ND QTR
3RD QTR
4TH QTR
TOTAL INCOME
TOTAL CANDIDATES

Display the seven courses together with the overall totals row in the first column.

WORD PROCESSING
DATABASES
SPREADSHEETS
DTP
BUSINESS APPLICATIONS
COMMUNICATIONS
CAD
OVERALL TOTALS

2 Enter the data. Using the appropriate formulae, generate the *total income* per course and the *total candidates* per course.

3 Save and print the spreadsheet.

4 Insert a column headed INCOME GROWTH before the TOTAL INCOME column, showing a growth of 5 per cent on the total income for each course.

5 Calculate the overall totals for the relevant columns and print two copies of the spreadsheet - the first printout to show *all figures* and the second to show the *formulae* for the OVERALL TOTALS for TOTAL CANDIDATES, INCOME GROWTH and TOTAL INCOME.

6 To determine the additional profit which would be made if the income growth was in fact 10 per cent, make the relevant change and print OVERALL TOTALS for TOTAL CANDIDATES, INCOME GROWTH and TOTAL INCOME.

WORD PROCESSING

Create a file using a 65 column line length (or 6.5" if you are using proportional spacing), single line spacing and a justified right-hand margin. Enter the text below, number all pages, save and print.

BALFOUR SEMINARS } ← Centre and embolden
ANNUAL REPORT }

Underline all sub headings

Introduction

Balfour Seminars was established 5 years ago by Jenny Price, a full-time lecturer in Computing at Southwood College of F.E. Jenny had developed an interest in preparing training courses and the relevant teaching materials. She decided to take a risk and move into the training field on a full-time basis by establishing her own business. With a small amount of personal capital and a bank loan, she converted a small shop with living quarters above into a training agency. The first 3 months were spent in ~~setting~~ developing the materials, setting up the equipment as well as decorating the new premises. The courses to be offered initially were Word Processing, Spreadsheets and Databases and during the next 12 months 115 students were trained. Business steadily increased and the following graph shows the number of students trained last year.

Start new page.

Range of Applications/Packages

It soon became obvious that the range of packages on offer needed to be increased. By the end of the first year, 4 different word processing programs and 2 different spreadsheet and database programs were on offer.

In the second year, Jenny ~~also~~ decided to try to extend the range of applications on offer, but realised that if this part of the venture was to be successful she would need to bring in additional help. She canvassed her ex-colleagues and contacts to find those who would be prepared to work with her on a "when needed" basis.

By the end of the 3rd year the courses on offer had been increased as follows:

Application		No of Programs	Venues
WP	Type in full	5	5
DB		5	4
SS		3	3
DTP		3	3
CAD		2	2
B App		6	5
Comms		2	1

Venues (This section in double line sp)

As can be seen from the above table, there are now a number of venues on offer. Jenny advertised in one of the computer magazines offering set courses at set times. The response was good. The courses were offered in good hotels with seminar facilities - the equipment being carried and set up as and when required. If the initiative continues to expand, Jenny intends to rent permanent premises in a number of cities.

Payment

Courses can be paid for either by Cheque, Purchase Order or Credit Card. Business improved when courses were offered with payment by credit card. This was tried first of all in Liverpool where DTP had had no takers. The following shows the number of delegates who paid for their DTP courses by credit card.

Leave 1"

As a result, this facility was extended to all courses.

Income

The cost of the courses has remained static over the past 2 years, whereas the costs have increased. Jenny has decided to increase the prices of the courses, and has discovered that a 10% increase would result in the following figures:

Leave 1½"

An increase in income would mean that more up to date machines could be purchased.

The Future

The Company has grown considerably since its first students 5 years ago, and plans have been made to increase the turnover even more. These include:

- permanent premises in 10 cities
- a full-time trainer in charge of each centre
- bespoke training
- expansion into other areas of training
- publication of materials.

GRAPHICS

1 Using the data supplied, prepare and label a chart showing the numbers taking the different courses.

You may use either a pie chart or a bar chart or histogram.

2 Use the heading - COURSES

3 Save and print the display.

COLLATING THE INFORMATION

1 Recall the word processing file.

2 *Either* insert the graph which you have created for the numbers of trainees on courses at the end of the first page, *or* convert an additional printout into Appendix A and place it at the end of the document. Remember to make an appropriate note in the text of the word processed document.

3 After the paragraph commencing 'Courses can be paid ...' insert the extract from the database, ie

Those students who enrolled for DTP courses in Liverpool paying by credit card.

4 After the paragraph commencing 'The cost of the courses ...', insert the extract from the spreadsheet assignment (step 6), ie

The totals showing the 10 per cent increase in income growth.

5 Renumber and repaginate the document as required.

6 Present the final document.

NOTE:

The spreadsheet and database extracts must not be rekeyed. They should be included using:

(a) an integrated package
(b) separate printouts which have been cut and pasted, or
(c) desktop publishing.

BALFOUR SEMINARS – DATA SHEET

BALFOUR SEMINARS
Quarterly Figures
Quarter: First

Course	Cost	Candidates
WP	£105	76
DB	£100	50
SS	£110	63
DTP	£125	58
Bus Apps	£115	15
Comms	£130	12
CAD	£130	7

BALFOUR SEMINARS
Quarterly Figures
Quarter: Second

Course	Cost	Candidates
WP	£105	100
DB	£100	90
SS	£110	59
DTP	£125	41
Bus Apps	£115	17
Comms	£130	9
CAD	£130	15

BALFOUR SEMINARS
Quarterly Figures
Quarter: Third

Course	Cost	Candidates
WP	£105	50
DB	£100	67
SS	£110	74
DTP	£125	53
Bus Apps	£115	21
Comms	£130	15
CAD	£130	19

BALFOUR SEMINARS
Quarterly Figures
Quarter: Fourth

Course	Cost	Candidates
WP	£105	125
DB	£100	109
SS	£110	86
DTP	£125	62
Bus Apps	£115	18
Comms	£130	14
CAD	£130	23

BALFOUR SEMINARS – ENROLMENT FORMS

BALFOUR SEMINARS
ENROLMENT FORM
RING first - CONFIRM next

Confirmation No: 101

COURSE
- ☐ Word Processing (WP 761)
- ☐ Databases (DB 762)
- ☐ Spreadsheets (SS 763)
- ☑ Desk Top Publishing (DTP 764)
- ☐ Business Applications (BA 765)
- ☐ Communications (CO 766)
- ☐ C A D (CAD 767)

VENUE
- ☐ London
- ☐ Leeds
- ☑ Liverpool
- ☐ Manchester
- ☐ Birmingham
- ☐ Glasgow
- ☐ Newcastle

Delegate's Name: JOHNSTONE, ANNE
Company Address: Philips Electronics
Central Ave.
Southport SP6 2TQ
Daytime Tel No: 627516

METHOD OF PAYMENT
- ☐ A cheque for £ is enclosed.
- ☐ Purchase Order No enclosed.
- ☑ Charge the following Credit Card: Access/~~Visa/AMEX~~

No: 5224 9876 1432 8621
with the sum of £ 125 Expiry date: 07/93
Signature: A Johnstone

BALFOUR SEMINARS
ENROLMENT FORM
RING first - CONFIRM next

Confirmation No: 106

COURSE
- ☐ Word Processing (WP 761)
- ☑ Databases (DB 762)
- ☐ Spreadsheets (SS 763)
- ☐ Desk Top Publishing (DTP 764)
- ☐ Business Applications (BA 765)
- ☐ Communications (CO 766)
- ☐ C A D (CAD 767)

VENUE
- ☑ London
- ☐ Leeds
- ☐ Liverpool
- ☐ Manchester
- ☐ Birmingham
- ☐ Glasgow
- ☐ Newcastle

Delegate's Name: EDGE, Joan
Company Address: Philips Electronics
Central Ave.
Southport SP6 2TQ
Daytime Tel No: 627516

METHOD OF PAYMENT
- ☐ A cheque for £ is enclosed.
- ☑ Purchase Order No 62514 enclosed.
- ☐ Charge the following Credit Card: Access/Visa/AMEX

No:
with the sum of £ 100 Expiry date:
Signature: J Edge

BALFOUR SEMINARS
ENROLMENT FORM
RING first - CONFIRM next

Confirmation No: 112

COURSE	VENUE
☐ Word Processing (WP 761)	☐ London
☐ Databases (DB 762)	☑ Leeds
☑ Spreadsheets (SS 763)	☐ Liverpool
☐ Desk Top Publishing (DTP 764)	☐ Manchester
☐ Business Applications (BA 765)	☐ Birmingham
☐ Communications (CO 766)	☐ Glasgow
☐ C A D (CAD 767)	☐ Newcastle

Delegate's Name: PURCELL, VERA
Company Address: Grant Enterprises
Grantby Indus. Est.
Grantby Leeds
Daytime Tel No: 522 6000

METHOD OF PAYMENT
☑ A cheque for £ 110 is enclosed.
☐ Purchase Order No enclosed.
☐ Charge the following Credit Card: Access/Visa/AMEX
No:
with the sum of £ Expiry date:
Signature: V Purcell

BALFOUR SEMINARS
ENROLMENT FORM
RING first - CONFIRM next

Confirmation No: 109

COURSE	VENUE
☐ Word Processing (WP 761)	☐ London
☐ Databases (DB 762)	☐ Leeds
☐ Spreadsheets (SS 763)	☐ Liverpool
☐ Desk Top Publishing (DTP 764)	☑ Manchester
☐ Business Applications (BA 765)	☐ Birmingham
☑ Communications (CO 766)	☐ Glasgow
☐ C A D (CAD 767)	☐ Newcastle

Delegate's Name: MARSDEN Philip
Company Address: ACE Electronics plc
Electronics House
Somer St. M/C
Daytime Tel No: 616 8752

METHOD OF PAYMENT
☐ A cheque for £ is enclosed.
☐ Purchase Order No enclosed.
☑ Charge the following Credit Card: ~~Access~~/Visa/~~AMEX~~
No: 627 165 432 892
with the sum of £ 130 Expiry date: 04/93
Signature: Philip Marsden

BALFOUR SEMINARS
ENROLMENT FORM
RING first - CONFIRM next

Confirmation No: 117

COURSE
- ❑ Word Processing (WP 761)
- ❑ Databases (DB 762)
- ❑ Spreadsheets (SS 763)
- ❑ Desk Top Publishing (DTP 764)
- ❑ Business Applications (BA 765)
- ❑ Communications (CO 766)
- ☑ C A D (CAD 767)

VENUE
- ☑ London
- ❑ Leeds
- ❑ Liverpool
- ❑ Manchester
- ❑ Birmingham
- ❑ Glasgow
- ❑ Newcastle

Delegate's Name: MARSDEN Philip

Company Address: ACE Electronics plc
Electronics House
Somer St. M/C

Daytime Tel No: 616 8752

METHOD OF PAYMENT

❑ A cheque for £ is enclosed.

☑ Purchase Order No 24872 enclosed.

❑ Charge the following Credit Card: Access/Visa/AMEX

No:

with the sum of £ Expiry date:

Signature: Philip Marsden

BALFOUR SEMINARS
ENROLMENT FORM
RING first - CONFIRM next

Confirmation No: 104

COURSE
- ☑ Word Processing (WP 761)
- ❑ Databases (DB 762)
- ❑ Spreadsheets (SS 763)
- ❑ Desk Top Publishing (DTP 764)
- ❑ Business Applications (BA 765)
- ❑ Communications (CO 766)
- ❑ C A D (CAD 767)

VENUE
- ❑ London
- ❑ Leeds
- ❑ Liverpool
- ❑ Manchester
- ☑ Birmingham
- ❑ Glasgow
- ❑ Newcastle

Delegate's Name: JOHNSTONE, Anne

Company Address: Philips Electronics
Central Avenue.
Southport

Daytime Tel No: 627516

METHOD OF PAYMENT

☑ A cheque for £ 105 is enclosed.

❑ Purchase Order No enclosed.

❑ Charge the following Credit Card: Access/Visa/AMEX

No:

with the sum of £ Expiry date:

Signature: A Johnstone

BALFOUR SEMINARS
ENROLMENT FORM
RING first - CONFIRM next

Confirmation No: 119

COURSE
- ❑ Word Processing (WP 761)
- ❑ Databases (DB 762)
- ❑ Spreadsheets (SS 763)
- ☑ Desk Top Publishing (DTP 764)
- ❑ Business Applications (BA 765)
- ❑ Communications (CO 766)
- ❑ C A D (CAD 767)

VENUE
- ❑ London
- ❑ Leeds
- ☑ Liverpool
- ❑ Manchester
- ❑ Birmingham
- ❑ Glasgow
- ❑ Newcastle

Delegate's Name: TRACEY, Thomas
Company Address: Tracey Publications
27 Grosvenor Square
Liverpool
Daytime Tel No: 3219191

METHOD OF PAYMENT
- ❑ A cheque for £ is enclosed.
- ❑ Purchase Order No enclosed.
- ☑ Charge the following Credit Card: ~~Access/Visa~~/AMEX

No: 627 525 8061 2311
with the sum of £125 Expiry date: 09/94
Signature: Thomas Tracey

BALFOUR SEMINARS
ENROLMENT FORM
RING first - CONFIRM next

Confirmation No: 113

COURSE
- ☑ Word Processing (WP 761)
- ❑ Databases (DB 762)
- ❑ Spreadsheets (SS 763)
- ❑ Desk Top Publishing (DTP 764)
- ❑ Business Applications (BA 765)
- ❑ Communications (CO 766)
- ❑ C A D (CAD 767)

VENUE
- ❑ London
- ❑ Leeds
- ❑ Liverpool
- ❑ Manchester
- ❑ Birmingham
- ☑ Glasgow
- ❑ Newcastle

Delegate's Name: ALEXANDER Leslie
Company Address: Laptop Computing
Laptop House
Keen Street
Glasgow
Daytime Tel No: 387 2121

METHOD OF PAYMENT
- ❑ A cheque for £ is enclosed.
- ☑ Purchase Order No 61612 enclosed.
- ❑ Charge the following Credit Card: Access/Visa/AMEX

No:
with the sum of £ Expiry date:
Signature: Leslie Alexander

BALFOUR SEMINARS
ENROLMENT FORM
RING first - CONFIRM next

Confirmation No: 107

COURSE
- ☐ Word Processing (WP 761)
- ☐ Databases (DB 762)
- ☐ Spreadsheets (SS 763)
- ☐ Desk Top Publishing (DTP 764)
- ☑ Business Applications (BA 765)
- ☐ Communications (CO 766)
- ☐ C A D (CAD 767)

VENUE
- ☐ London
- ☐ Leeds
- ☐ Liverpool
- ☑ Manchester
- ☐ Birmingham
- ☐ Glasgow
- ☐ Newcastle

Delegate's Name: PETERSON, Geraldine
Company Address: Dan Instructors
City House
City Road
M/r
Daytime Tel No: 556 1739

METHOD OF PAYMENT
- ☑ A cheque for £ 115 is enclosed.
- ☐ Purchase Order No enclosed.
- ☐ Charge the following Credit Card: Access/Visa/AMEX

No:
with the sum of £ Expiry date:
Signature: G Peterson

BALFOUR SEMINARS
ENROLMENT FORM
RING first - CONFIRM next

Confirmation No: 115

COURSE
- ☑ Word Processing (WP 761)
- ☐ Databases (DB 762)
- ☐ Spreadsheets (SS 763)
- ☐ Desk Top Publishing (DTP 764)
- ☐ Business Applications (BA 765)
- ☐ Communications (CO 766)
- ☐ C A D (CAD 767)

VENUE
- ☑ London
- ☐ Leeds
- ☐ Liverpool
- ☐ Manchester
- ☐ Birmingham
- ☐ Glasgow
- ☐ Newcastle

Delegate's Name: HENDERSON, Stephen
Company Address: 27 Anstruther St.
London
W12 8QT
Daytime Tel No: 511 8796

METHOD OF PAYMENT
- ☐ A cheque for £ is enclosed.
- ☐ Purchase Order No enclosed.
- ☑ Charge the following Credit Card: Access/~~Visa/AMEX~~

No: 621 387 426 526
with the sum of £ 105 Expiry date: 10/94
Signature: S. Henderson

BALFOUR SEMINARS
ENROLMENT FORM
RING first - CONFIRM next

Confirmation No: 102

COURSE
- ☐ Word Processing (WP 761)
- ☐ Databases (DB 762)
- ☑ Spreadsheets (SS 763)
- ☐ Desk Top Publishing (DTP 764)
- ☐ Business Applications (BA 765)
- ☐ Communications (CO 766)
- ☐ C A D (CAD 767)

VENUE
- ☐ London
- ☐ Leeds
- ☐ Liverpool
- ☐ Manchester
- ☐ Birmingham
- ☐ Glasgow
- ☑ Newcastle

Delegate's Name: ANDREWS Carol

Company Address: N E Breweries
Brewery House
Newcastle

Daytime Tel No: 386 2812

METHOD OF PAYMENT
- ☐ A cheque for £ is enclosed.
- ☑ Purchase Order No 274 enclosed.
- ☐ Charge the following Credit Card: Access/Visa/AMEX

No:

with the sum of £ Expiry date:

Signature: C Andrews

BALFOUR SEMINARS
ENROLMENT FORM
RING first - CONFIRM next

Confirmation No: 111

COURSE
- ☐ Word Processing (WP 761)
- ☑ Databases (DB 762)
- ☐ Spreadsheets (SS 763)
- ☐ Desk Top Publishing (DTP 764)
- ☐ Business Applications (BA 765)
- ☐ Communications (CO 766)
- ☐ C A D (CAD 767)

VENUE
- ☑ London
- ☐ Leeds
- ☐ Liverpool
- ☐ Manchester
- ☐ Birmingham
- ☐ Glasgow
- ☐ Newcastle

Delegate's Name: KIRBY, ANDREW

Company Address: ASite + KIRBY
97 Strong Street
London W1S 9TZ

Daytime Tel No: 446 2192

METHOD OF PAYMENT
- ☐ A cheque for £ is enclosed.
- ☑ Purchase Order No 66625 enclosed.
- ☐ Charge the following Credit Card: Access/Visa/AMEX

No:

with the sum of £ Expiry date:

Signature: A Kirby

BALFOUR SEMINARS

ENROLMENT FORM

RING first - CONFIRM next

Confirmation No: 120

COURSE	VENUE
❑ Word Processing (WP 761)	❑ London
❑ Databases (DB 762)	❑ Leeds
❑ Spreadsheets (SS 763)	❑ Liverpool
❑ Desk Top Publishing (DTP 764)	☑ Manchester
☑ Business Applications (BA 765)	❑ Birmingham
❑ Communications (CO 766)	❑ Glasgow
❑ C A D (CAD 767)	❑ Newcastle

Delegate's Name: CROSBY, Anthony

Company Address: CAB Petroleum
Petroleum House
10 The Causeway M/r

Daytime Tel No: 323 8616

METHOD OF PAYMENT

☑ A cheque for £ 115 is enclosed.

❑ Purchase Order No enclosed.

❑ Charge the following Credit Card: Access/Visa/AMEX

No:

with the sum of £ Expiry date:

Signature: A Crosby

BALFOUR SEMINARS

ENROLMENT FORM

RING first - CONFIRM next

Confirmation No: 108

COURSE	VENUE
☑ Word Processing (WP 761)	❑ London
❑ Databases (DB 762)	❑ Leeds
❑ Spreadsheets (SS 763)	❑ Liverpool
❑ Desk Top Publishing (DTP 764)	❑ Manchester
❑ Business Applications (BA 765)	☑ Birmingham
❑ Communications (CO 766)	❑ Glasgow
❑ C A D (CAD 767)	❑ Newcastle

Delegate's Name: PETERSON Geraldine

Company Address: Dean Instructors
City House
City Road
M/r

Daytime Tel No: 556 1739

METHOD OF PAYMENT

❑ A cheque for £ is enclosed.

☑ Purchase Order No 126 enclosed.

❑ Charge the following Credit Card: Access/Visa/AMEX

No:

with the sum of £ Expiry date:

Signature: G Peterson

BALFOUR SEMINARS
ENROLMENT FORM
RING first - CONFIRM next

Confirmation No: 116

COURSE
- ☐ Word Processing (WP 761)
- ☑ Databases (DB 762)
- ☐ Spreadsheets (SS 763)
- ☐ Desk Top Publishing (DTP 764)
- ☐ Business Applications (BA 765)
- ☐ Communications (CO 766)
- ☐ C A D (CAD 767)

VENUE
- ☐ London
- ☐ Leeds
- ☐ Liverpool
- ☐ Manchester
- ☐ Birmingham
- ☑ Glasgow
- ☐ Newcastle

Delegate's Name: TERRY, GERALD
Company Address: Terry Engineering
62 Claughton St.
Glasgow
Daytime Tel No: 862 1437

METHOD OF PAYMENT
- ☑ A cheque for £ 100 is enclosed.
- ☐ Purchase Order No enclosed.
- ☐ Charge the following Credit Card: Access/Visa/AMEX

No:
with the sum of £ Expiry date:
Signature: G Terry

BALFOUR SEMINARS
ENROLMENT FORM
RING first - CONFIRM next

Confirmation No: 103

COURSE
- ☐ Word Processing (WP 761)
- ☐ Databases (DB 762)
- ☑ Spreadsheets (SS 763)
- ☐ Desk Top Publishing (DTP 764)
- ☐ Business Applications (BA 765)
- ☐ Communications (CO 766)
- ☐ C A D (CAD 767)

VENUE
- ☑ London
- ☐ Leeds
- ☐ Liverpool
- ☐ Manchester
- ☐ Birmingham
- ☐ Glasgow
- ☐ Newcastle

Delegate's Name: GOSWORTH Jonathan
Company Address: BRIDGE (UK) LTD
Anderson Ind. Est.
Anderson W19 7PQ
Daytime Tel No: 717 8672

METHOD OF PAYMENT
- ☐ A cheque for £ is enclosed.
- ☑ Purchase Order No 5161 enclosed.
- ☐ Charge the following Credit Card: Access/Visa/AMEX

No:
with the sum of £ Expiry date:
Signature: J Gosworth

BALFOUR SEMINARS
ENROLMENT FORM
RING first - CONFIRM next

Confirmation No: 118

COURSE
- ☐ Word Processing (WP 761)
- ☐ Databases (DB 762)
- ☐ Spreadsheets (SS 763)
- ☑ Desk Top Publishing (DTP 764)
- ☐ Business Applications (BA 765)
- ☐ Communications (CO 766)
- ☐ C A D (CAD 767)

VENUE
- ☐ London
- ☐ Leeds
- ☑ Liverpool
- ☐ Manchester
- ☐ Birmingham
- ☐ Glasgow
- ☐ Newcastle

Delegate's Name: WALSALL, Jennifer
Company Address: 62 Anderson Terrace
Liverpool
Daytime Tel No: 222 8753

METHOD OF PAYMENT
- ☐ A cheque for £ is enclosed.
- ☐ Purchase Order No enclosed.
- ☑ Charge the following Credit Card: Access/~~Visa/AMEX~~

No: 617 825 256 143
with the sum of £ 125 Expiry date: 01/95
Signature: J Walsall

BALFOUR SEMINARS
ENROLMENT FORM
RING first - CONFIRM next

Confirmation No: 110

COURSE
- ☐ Word Processing (WP 761)
- ☐ Databases (DB 762)
- ☑ Spreadsheets (SS 763)
- ☐ Desk Top Publishing (DTP 764)
- ☐ Business Applications (BA 765)
- ☐ Communications (CO 766)
- ☐ C A D (CAD 767)

VENUE
- ☐ London
- ☐ Leeds
- ☐ Liverpool
- ☐ Manchester
- ☑ Birmingham
- ☐ Glasgow
- ☐ Newcastle

Delegate's Name: RICHMOND Elizabeth
Company Address: Richmond Fashions
35 Spark St.
B'ham
Daytime Tel No: 414 2019

METHOD OF PAYMENT
- ☑ A cheque for £ 110 is enclosed.
- ☐ Purchase Order No enclosed.
- ☐ Charge the following Credit Card: Access/Visa/AMEX

No:
with the sum of £ Expiry date:
Signature: E Richmond

BALFOUR SEMINARS
ENROLMENT FORM
RING first - CONFIRM next

Confirmation No: 114

COURSE	VENUE
☑ Word Processing (WP 761)	☐ London
☐ Databases (DB 762)	☐ Leeds
☐ Spreadsheets (SS 763)	☑ Liverpool
☐ Desk Top Publishing (DTP 764)	☐ Manchester
☐ Business Applications (BA 765)	☐ Birmingham
☐ Communications (CO 766)	☐ Glasgow
☐ C A D (CAD 767)	☐ Newcastle

Delegate's Name: LOWE Christine
Company Address: Carters Papers
Unit 21
Brindley Ind. Est.
Liv.
Daytime Tel No: 534 0978

METHOD OF PAYMENT
☐ A cheque for £ is enclosed.
☑ Purchase Order No 227 enclosed.
☐ Charge the following Credit Card: Access/Visa/AMEX
No:
with the sum of £ Expiry date:
Signature: C Lowe

BALFOUR SEMINARS
ENROLMENT FORM
RING first - CONFIRM next

Confirmation No: 105

COURSE	VENUE
☑ Word Processing (WP 761)	☐ London
☐ Databases (DB 762)	☐ Leeds
☐ Spreadsheets (SS 763)	☐ Liverpool
☐ Desk Top Publishing (DTP 764)	☐ Manchester
☐ Business Applications (BA 765)	☑ Birmingham
☐ Communications (CO 766)	☐ Glasgow
☐ C A D (CAD 767)	☐ Newcastle

Delegate's Name: HARTLEY, Teresa
Company Address: Dan Instructors
City House
City Road
M/r
Daytime Tel No: 556 1739

METHOD OF PAYMENT
☑ A cheque for £ 105 is enclosed.
☐ Purchase Order No enclosed.
☐ Charge the following Credit Card: Access/Visa/AMEX
No:
with the sum of £ Expiry date:
Signature: T. Hartley

ASSIGNMENT 2

DATABASE

1 As clerk for Balfour Stamps, you have been asked to set up a database for the stock check of stamps which is carried out every six months. Set up the database using the following fields:

REF
TYPE
YEAR
DESCRIPTION
UNMOUNTED MINT (abbreviate to UMM)
MOUNTED MINT (abbreviate to MM)
VERY FINE USED (abbreviate to VFU)
USED (abbreviate to U)

2 Enter the data from the stock check sheets (pages 142 - 51) into the relevant fields putting the number of stamps in stock in the fields UMM, MM, VFU and U.

3 Save the data.

4 Print the data.

5 Sort the list into ascending numerical order of REF.

6 Save the sorted list and print one copy.

7 Using the search facility, find the unmounted mint commemorative stamps issued since 1970 with a *stock of less than 1000.*

8 Save and print the list generated from the search, showing REF, YEAR, DESCRIPTION and PRICE.

SPREADSHEET

1 Using the details on the stock check sheets (pages 142 - 51) create a spreadsheet using the title BALFOUR STAMPS STOCK CHECK.

Use the following column headings:

DESCRIPTION
REF
UMM
VALUE
MM
VALUE
TOTAL VALUE

List the description of the eleven *commemorative* stamps in the first column in the following order:

COUNCIL
DARWIN
GEOGRAPHICAL
JUBILEE
LIFEBOAT
MARITIME
PUC £1
ROYAL MAIL
SHAKESPEARE
UNIVERSITIES
WEMBLEY

2 Extract the relevant data from the cards and enter it on to the spreadsheet. Use the appropriate formulae to generate the stock value of each item for unmounted and mounted mint. Use a formula to calculate the total value of *all* stock for each item.

3 Save and print one copy.

4 Insert a column headed PROJECTED VALUE *before* MM. Use a formula in this column to show the effect of a 10 per cent price increase for UMM stock.

5 Calculate the TOTAL for *all* VALUE columns. Save and print two copies of the spreadsheet - the first should show the figures and the second should show the formulae for the totals of *all* values.

6 Show the change to the PROJECTED VALUE column of an increase of 15 per cent. Print the totals for all values and include the column headings in your printout.

WORD PROCESSING

Create a file using a 65 column line length (or 6.5" if you are using proportional spacing), single line spacing and a justified right-hand margin. Enter the text below, number all pages, save and print.

BALFOUR STAMPS
AUTUMN NEWSLETTER } Centre and Embolden

The management of Balfour Stamps is keen to keep its customers up to date and well informed. With this in mind, we intend to produce a newsletter four times a year which will be sent to all ~~of our~~ customers on our mailing list. This will contain items of interest to all stamp collectors and features articles on unusual aspects of your hobby.

Stocks (Underscore all side headings)

We currently hold a very large stock of all types of stamps - commemoratives, definitives, postage dues etc. in varying conditions. The better the condition of the stamp the higher, in general, will be the price. [For our special offers this month we have selected eleven of the unmounted mint versions of our large stock of commemoratives. The following graph shows the numbers we had in stock at 30 June of each of these sets.

New page here.

The stock of commemorative sets at any one time within the company is normally in excess of 1500, but recently there has been an increased demand for items from 1970 onwards. In May we offered a number of sets for sale at very reduced prices and consequently our stocks have been diminished. The following shows the stock levels as at 30 June.

Leave 1½"

As can be seen a number of the sets have now dropped below the level of 1000. Consequently we are now looking for further supplies.

Stamps as an Investment

Stamp collectors have many different reasons for collecting - whatever the reason most people like to see their investment grow. Stamp collecting can be an expensive hobby with some stamps costing hundreds of pounds each.

The value of the stamp depends upon its rarity and quality. The more stamps issued, the less likely they are to become rarities. However, it is still possible to see a reasonable return over a number of years. For example, a 15% increase in price would have the following effect on the price of unmounted mint:

Leave 1"

What are Composites?

A recent venture in the production of new issues of stamps is the Composite. The design is spread over more than one stamp, there is no margin and the design is devised in such a way that each stamp is a picture in its own right. The first was issued in Poland in 1957. It has been used by a number of countries since then, for instance in 1989 Guernsey presented its Xmas stamps in the form of 9 stamps making up a Xmas tree. A number of composite issues have been produced using the Walt Disney Cartoon Character themes.

Thematics (This section in double line spacing)

A popular form of collecting today is Thematic. A theme is chosen and stamps from all over the world depicting that theme are collected. Birds, animals, trains and flowers are just a few of the common themes. I heard a story last week of a man who had Penguins as his theme - needless to say, his collection was not very large.

Send for our thematic lists.

Exhibitions

The Exhibition Programme over the next 6 months is as follows:

Date	Venue
3 July	Warrington
4 Aug	Birmingham
17 Aug	Liverpool
4 Sep.	Manchester
12 Oct	Crewe
10 Nov	Bolton
21 Nov	Wrexham
6 Dec	Liverpool
19 Dec	Blackpool

GRAPHICS

1 Using the stock check sheets (pages 142 - 51), create and label a graph showing the current stock for the commemorative issues of mounted mint stamps.

Use the title:

MOUNTED MINT - COMMEMORATIVES

2 Save the graph.

3 Print the graph.

COLLATING THE INFORMATION

1 Recall the word processing assignment file.

2 *Either* insert the graph which you have created for the stock of MOUNTED MINT COMMEMORATIVES at the end of the first page, *or* convert an additional printout into Appendix A and place it at the end of the document. Remember to make an appropriate note in the text of the word processed document.

3 After the paragraph on page 2 starting 'The stock of commemorative sets ...' insert the extract from the database assignment (page 135), ie

The commemorative stamps issued since 1970 with an unmounted mint stock of less than 1000.

4 At the end of the section on Stamps as an Investment, insert the extract from the spreadsheet assignment step 6 (page 136), ie

The totals of all values plus the relevant headings.

5 Renumber and repaginate the document as required.

6 Present the final document.

NOTE:

The spreadsheet and database extracts must not be rekeyed. They should be included using

(a) an integrated package, or
(b) separate printouts which have been cut and pasted, or
(c) desktop publishing.

BALFOUR STAMP COMPANY – STOCK CHECK

BALFOUR STAMP COMPANY

STOCK CHECK

AS AT 30th JUNE

Reference No: 279

Type: Commemorative

Year: 1963

Description: Lifeboats

	NO IN STOCK	PRICE
Unmounted Mint	1011	£ 1.90
Mounted Mint	2015	£ 2.10
Very Fine Used	876	£ 2.00
Used	1313	£ 1.25

BALFOUR STAMP COMPANY

STOCK CHECK

AS AT 30th JUNE

Reference No: 364

Type: Postage Due

Year: 1914

Description: Royal Cypher

	NO IN STOCK	PRICE
Unmounted Mint	406	£ 165.00
Mounted Mint	217	£ 105.00
Very Fine Used	363	£ 19.50
Used	181	£ 11.75

BALFOUR STAMP COMPANY
STOCK CHECK
AS AT 30th JUNE

Reference No: 425
Type: Commemorative
Year: 1982
Description: Darwin

	NO IN STOCK	PRICE
Unmounted Mint	611	£ 1.00
Mounted Mint	322	£ .90
Very Fine Used	481	£ .80
Used	379	£ .60

BALFOUR STAMP COMPANY
STOCK CHECK
AS AT 30th JUNE

Reference No: 290
Type: Définitives
Year: 1918
Description: Seahorses

	NO IN STOCK	PRICE
Unmounted Mint	56	£ 375.00
Mounted Mint	34	£ 225.00
Very Fine Used	42	£ 65.00
Used	21	£ 20.00

BALFOUR STAMP COMPANY
STOCK CHECK
AS AT 30th JUNE

Reference No: 345

Type: Commemoratives

Year: 1982

Description: Maritime

	NO IN STOCK	PRICE
Unmounted Mint	1275	£ 1.30
Mounted Mint	1074	£ 1.30
Very Fine Used	862	£ 1.00
Used	309	£ .70

BALFOUR STAMP COMPANY
STOCK CHECK
AS AT 30th JUNE

Reference No: 451

Type: Commemorative

Year: 1929

Description: PUC £1

	NO IN STOCK	PRICE
Unmounted Mint	20	£ 495.00
Mounted Mint	15	£ 385.00
Very Fine Used	17	£ 310.00
Used	12	£ 225.00

BALFOUR STAMP COMPANY
STOCK CHECK
AS AT 30th JUNE

Reference No: 287
Type: Postage Due
Year: 1937
Description: George VI

	NO IN STOCK	PRICE
Unmounted Mint	92	£ 100.00
Mounted Mint	63	£ 62.50
Very Fine Used	49	£ 12.50
Used	83	£ 7.25

BALFOUR STAMP COMPANY
STOCK CHECK
AS AT 30th JUNE

Reference No: 387
Type: Definitives
Year: 1915
Description: Seahorses

	NO IN STOCK	PRICE
Unmounted Mint	10	£1250.00
Mounted Mint	9	£ 875.00
Very Fine Used	12	£ 300.00
Used	16	£ 75.00

BALFOUR STAMP COMPANY
STOCK CHECK
AS AT 30th JUNE

Reference No: 400
Type: Commemorative
Year: 1924
Description: Wembley

	NO IN STOCK	PRICE
Unmounted Mint	863	£ 11.50
Mounted Mint	773	£ 9.00
Very Fine Used	312	£ 6.50
Used	800	£ 7.00

BALFOUR STAMP COMPANY
STOCK CHECK
AS AT 30th JUNE

Reference No: 361
Type: Definitives
Year: 1887
Description: Jubilee

	NO IN STOCK	PRICE
Unmounted Mint	130	£ 295.00
Mounted Mint	364	£ 140.00
Very Fine Used	79	£ 59.00
Used	135	£ 24.00

BALFOUR STAMP COMPANY
STOCK CHECK
AS AT 30th JUNE

Reference No: 332
Type: Commemoratives
Year: 1984
Description: Royal Mail

	NO IN STOCK	PRICE
Unmounted Mint	1187	£ 1.80
Mounted Mint	901	£ 1.50
Very Fine Used	842	£ 1.30
Used	996	£ 1.30

BALFOUR STAMP COMPANY
STOCK CHECK
AS AT 30th JUNE

Reference No: 491
Type: Postage Due
Year: 1955
Description: Edward

	NO IN STOCK	PRICE
Unmounted Mint	49	£ 200.00
Mounted Mint	36	£ 105.00
Very Fine Used	170	£ ·10.50
Used	204	£ 23.00

BALFOUR STAMP COMPANY
STOCK CHECK
AS AT 30th JUNE

Reference No: 262
Type: Definitives
Year: 1934
Description: Seahorses

	NO IN STOCK	PRICE
Unmounted Mint	38	£ 380.00
Mounted Mint	17	£ 225.00
Very Fine Used	210	£ 35.00
Used	312	£ 19.00

BALFOUR STAMP COMPANY
STOCK CHECK
AS AT 30th JUNE

Reference No: 365
Type: Commemorative
Year: 1984
Description: Council

	NO IN STOCK	PRICE
Unmounted Mint	900	£ 1.80
Mounted Mint	812	£ 1.50
Very Fine Used	617	£ 1.30
Used	29	£ 1.00

BALFOUR STAMP COMPANY
STOCK CHECK
AS AT 30th JUNE

Reference No: 436
Type: Definitives
Year: 1913
Description: Seahorses

	NO IN STOCK	PRICE
Unmounted Mint	12	£ 1800.00
Mounted Mint	10	£ 1200.00
Very Fine Used	9	£ 700.00
Used	14	£ 325.00

BALFOUR STAMP COMPANY
STOCK CHECK
AS AT 30th JUNE

Reference No: 293
Type: Commemorative
Year: 1964
Description: Geographical

	NO IN STOCK	PRICE
Unmounted Mint	638	£ 4.10
Mounted Mint	504	£ 3.50
Very Fine Used	473	£ 3.00
Used	523	£ 2.10

BALFOUR STAMP COMPANY
STOCK CHECK
AS AT 30th JUNE

Reference No: 355
Type: Commemorative
Year: 1935
Description: Jubilee

	NO IN STOCK	PRICE
Unmounted Mint	721	£ 3.85
Mounted Mint	872	£ 3.75
Very Fine Used	912	£ 3.30
Used	451	£ 2.50

BALFOUR STAMP COMPANY
STOCK CHECK
AS AT 30th JUNE

Reference No: 422
Type: Commemorative
Year: 1964
Description: Shakespeare

	NO IN STOCK	PRICE
Unmounted Mint	313	£ 2.85
Mounted Mint	419	£ 2.55
Very Fine Used	657	£ 1.90
Used	878	£ 1.30

BALFOUR STAMP COMPANY
STOCK CHECK
AS AT 30th JUNE

Reference No: 373
Type: Postage Due
Year: 1970
Description: Decimals

	NO IN STOCK	PRICE
Unmounted Mint	100	£ 18.00
Mounted Mint	210	£ 15.00
Very Fine Used	481	£ 4.25
Used	561	£ 2.75

BALFOUR STAMP COMPANY
STOCK CHECK
AS AT 30th JUNE

Reference No: 411
Type: Commemoratives
Year: 1971
Description: Universities

	NO IN STOCK	PRICE
Unmounted Mint	76	£ 1.70
Mounted Mint	59	£ 1.55
Very Fine Used	362	£ 1.10
Used	393	£ .55

UNIT 6

COMMUNICATIONS

For this unit, you will need to know how to set up and use a communications link.

D O Y O U K N O W ?

How to open a communications channel?

How to transmit a message?

How to receive a message?

How to print the received message?

How to close a communications channel?

There is only one assignment included in this unit, it will give you some idea of the type of assignment which you can be given by your tutor. The assignments will vary according to the equipment in use in your centre.

HINTS AND TIPS

1 This assignment is set by your own tutors and will be assessed by watching you perform the procedures.

2 Make sure that you can perform them easily and accurately.

3 Do not forget to include in your assessment a copy of the received message. If this is not available, there is no proof that you have completed this assignment.

ASSIGNMENT

The following is a sample assignment of how to complete this unit.

1 Key in and save the following text using your word processing package:

```
COMMUNICATIONS

Communications is an increasingly vital part of the
modern business world.  Companies are using this
medium to communicate quickly and easily over a wide
area.  The documents that are transmitted may be
confidential urgent communications within a company.
Or communications may also be the use of a commercial
database to extract statistics.
```

2 SEND A FILE

This section could include a step by step instruction on how to send the file using your hardware and software. It could include setting up the baud rate etc. required by your system.

3 RECEIVE A FILE

This section could include step by step instructions as for (2) above, but this time giving instructions on how to receive a file.

4 PRINT A FILE

When the file has been received, and is available either on disk or on the screen, the procedure will be outlined for printing the copy which is required for the assessment.

5 CLOSE DOWN THE SYSTEM

This section could include step by step instructions on the procedure to follow for correctly closing down the system.

SYLLABUS

CANDIDATES MUST BE ABLE TO:

SECTION 1 – SET UP AND USE THE FACILITIES OF A DATABASE STRUCTURE

Assessment Objectives	*Performance Criteria*
1.1 SELECT the relevant data	(a) All required data included (b) Unrequired data not included
1.2 ENTER the record structure	(a) Appropriate no of fields for data
1.3 DETERMINE field description	(a) Field type correctly described (b) Field type appropriate for data
1.4 ENTER the data	(a) No more than 5 Data Entry Errors (b) Data entered in manner logical for sorting
1.5 SEARCH on 3 criteria to select subsets of data	(a) Correct selection of all (only) record(s) in subset
1.6 SORT data (alphabetic/numeric)	(a) Correct order
1.7 SAVE data	(a) Structure and data can be recalled at a later date
1.8 PRINT hard copy	(a) Required reports printed

SECTION 2 - CREATE AND USE A SPREADSHEET TO AID PROBLEM SOLVING

Assessment Objectives		*Performance Criteria*	
2.1	ANALYSE given information	(a)	Information analysed into individual categories 100% accurately
2.2	DETERMINE the cell description	(a)	Cells correctly described
		(b)	Cells relevant to data
2.3	ENTER the spreadsheet layout	(a)	Data laid out appropriately
		(b)	Figures right-justified
		(c)	Dates presented in integer format
		(d)	Monetary amounts presented to 2 decimal places
2.4	ENTER data into the spreadsheet	(a)	No more than 3 Data Entry Errors
2.5	GENERATE and APPLY formulae	(a)	Formulae used which generate specific results
		(b)	Formulae entered in appropriate positions.
2.6	INSERT columns/rows	(a)	Column/row inserted in correct position
2.7	GENERATE 'what if?' projections	(a)	Correct projections made
2.8	SAVE data	(a)	Spreadsheet and data can be recalled at a later date
2.9	PRINT the spreadsheet data	(a)	Exact cells required printed
2.10	PRINT the spreadsheet formulae	(a)	Formulae printed with indication of cell position

SECTION 3 – USE WORD PROCESSING FACILITIES TO PRODUCE A MULTI-PAGE DOCUMENT

Assessment Objectives	*Performance Criteria*
3.1 IMPLEMENT a document format	(a) Line length correct within 3 characters (b) Line-spacing and justification as instructed
3.2 ENTER the text for a document	(a) No more than 3 Data Entry Errors
3.3 USE emboldening	(a) All the portion indicated (but no more) emboldened
3.4 USE underlining	(a) All the portion indicated (but no more) underlined
3.5 CENTRE lines	(a) 'Acceptably' centred (ie over text or on page)
3.6 VARY the line spacing	(a) 'Single' and 'double' line spacing followed within tolerance of minor variations such as 3 and 5 lines to 1"
3.7 ALLOCATE vertical space from given measurements	(a) Space left not less than specified and not excessively greater (with due regard to position on the page)
3.8 PRESENT a table	(a) Items in a row aligned (b) Each column consistently displayed
3.9 NUMBER the pages	(a) Position of page number as instructed or, if no instruction, anywhere above or below text (b) Consistent position of page numbers
3.10 SAVE the document	(a) Document can be recalled at a later date
3.11 PRINT the document	(a) All printing on the page (b) Printing not crossing perforations (if continuous stationery used)

SECTION 4 - PRODUCE A GRAPHICAL REPRESENTATION OF NUMERICAL DATA

Assessment Objectives		*Performance Criteria*	
4.1	EXTRACT relevant figures from source information	(a)	Correct figures extracted
4.2	ENTER numeric data	(a)	Correct figures entered
4.3	ENTER labels	(a)	Appropriate text entered with no more than 3 Data Entry Errors
4.4	PRODUCE an appropriate graphical representation of the data	(a)	Differentiation clearly shown by the graphical representation
4.5	SAVE the data	(a)	Graphical representation can be recalled at a later date
4.6	PRINT the graphical representation	(a)	Hard copy printed

SECTION 5 - INSERT INFORMATION FROM A DATABASE, SPREADSHEET AND A GRAPHICAL REPRESENTATION INTO A WORD PROCESSED DOCUMENT

Assessment Objectives		*Performance Criteria*	
5.1	EXTRACT INFORMATION according to instructions (generated using Database, Spreadsheet, Word Processing and Graphics packages) for inclusion in a document	(a)	Required portions of the documents extracted as instructed
5.2	PRESENT information accurately in a specified sequence and to an appropriate layout	(a)	Extracted portions inserted or referenced in the correct place
		(b)	Spacing before and after inserted sections/references adequate but not excessive

Assessment Objectives	*Performance Criteria*
5.2 (continued)	(c) Page breaks positioned sensibly eg not after headings, not before the last line of a paragraph
	(d) Newly keyed-in material entered with no more than 2 Data Entry Errors
5.3 PRINT information for the final document	The final document presented by:
	(a) Using integrated software to collate the different sections and then printing; or (b) printing out the extracts SEPARATELY from the word processed document and then sticking them in at the appropriate places; or (c) using desktop publishing facilities

SECTION 6 – USE A COMMUNICATIONS CHANNEL

Assessment Objectives	*Performance Criteria*
6.1 OPEN a communications channel	(a) Entry (log on) procedures, as appropriate, observed
6.2 TRANSMIT a message	(a) Pre-stored or keyed-in message of any length sent from one terminal to another (locally or remotely)
6.3 RECEIVE a message	(a) Message of at least 50 words, received from another local/remote terminal
6.4 PRINT the received message	(a) Received message printed
6.5 CLOSE a communications channel	(a) Close down (log off) procedures, as appropriate, observed

NOTE: This syllabus is reproduced by kind permission of the RSA.

A048380